מסורה

ArtScroll Series®

Rabbi Nosson Scherman / Rabbi Meir Zlotowitz

General Editors

MAKING SENSE

RABBI YITZCHOK KIRZNER

Prepared for Publication by
Jeremy Kagan and Yonoson Rosenblum

Published by
Mesorah Publications, ltd

OF
SUFFERING

A JEWISH APPROACH

FIRST EDITION
First Impression … September 2002

Published and Distributed by
MESORAH PUBLICATIONS, LTD.
4401 Second Avenue / Brooklyn, N.Y 11232

Distributed in Europe by
LEHMANNS
Unit E, Viking Industrial Park
Rolling Mill Road
Jarrow, Tyne & Wear, NE32 3DP
England

Distributed in Australia and New Zealand by
GOLDS WORLD OF JUDAICA
3-13 William Street
Balaclava, Melbourne 3183
Victoria Australia

Distributed in Israel by
SIFRIATI / A. GITLER
6 Hayarkon Street
Bnei Brak 51127

Distributed in South Africa by
KOLLEL BOOKSHOP
Shop 8A Norwood Hypermarket
Norwood 2196, Johannesburg, South Africa

Typography by CompuScribe at ArtScroll Studios, Ltd.

Printed in the United States of America by Noble Book Press Corp.
Bound by Sefercraft, Quality Bookbinders, Ltd., Brooklyn N.Y. 11232

PREFACE

W E FAILED.

It was beyond our capacity to capture the experience of listening to Rabbi Yitzchak Kirzner, *zt"l*, on the printed page. Rabbi Kirzner was one of the great Torah teachers of our era. Even when discussing the most difficult and erudite subjects, he had a way of enveloping each and every listener in soothing warmth. He conveyed love with his voice and the twinkle in his eye. No one who had the experience of having his hand caressed by Rabbi Kirzner ever forgot the experience. That warmth and love we could not convey.

Of the thousands of classes that Rabbi Kirzner gave over a decade and a half, on every aspect of Jewish thought, these classes on responding to suffering held a particular urgency for him. At the time that he commenced this set of classes, he had already been diagnosed with the disease that would claim his life. In his introduction, he mentions, without elaborating, that he has "earned" the right to talk about suffering. That he surely had. In the course of this set of classes, he was undergoing painful and frequently debilitating treatments. That was known to many of his listeners, and surely added to the drama and impact of these classes, in a manner we have been unable to replicate.

One more disclaimer is in order. This book is not a literal transcription of Rabbi Kirzner's classes. The written word is not simply the spoken word put on page. Not even the most eloquent teacher – and Rabbi Kirzner was certainly eloquent – speaks in publishable sentences, unless he is reading from a prepared text. Rabbi Kirzner was too much the teacher to ever read a prepared text.

A successful lecture or class is an emotional experience as well as a means of conveying information, and something of that emotional impact is inevitably lost in writing. The written work, therefore, will be judged by a different standard entirely. Unlike those listening to a lecture, readers have the luxury of stopping at will to review the argument, and are therefore in a better position to judge the philosophical rigor of the presentation.

Mindful of that distinction, we have filled in missing half-steps in a few places, just as Rabbi Kirzner would surely have done had he lived to see his classes in print. (He intended to publish a book on the subject of suffering, and had, in fact, completed a first draft.) In addition, we have tried to provide many of the sources so that the reader who is interested will have an opportunity to examine for himself the vast range of classical sources upon which Rabbi Kirzner was drawing.

Because Rabbi Kirzner gave this series of classes over a period of time, he inevitably found it necessary to summarize the argument at the beginning of each new class. While we have retained many of those internal summaries, they have been trimmed out in consideration to readers, who will not be pausing for a week or more between each chapter. In addition, we have dropped much of the first-person presentation found in the lectures. Use of the first-person "I" is natural when the lecturer is present before the audience, but less so in a book whose author is no longer with us.

We are convinced that Rabbi Kirzner successfully distilled the major Torah teachings on reconciling human suffering with G-d's benevolence, and that this book will be of great assistance to anyone struggling with these issues.

Unfortunately, the issues raised by human suffering have become no less urgent than they were when Moses first broached the subject of the suffering of the righteous with G-d. Though we look forward to a redeemed world in which all human suffering has come to an end, until that day, it is our hope that Rabbi Kirzner's work will provide understanding and comfort for all those dealing with their own suffering or the suffering of those dear to them.

Jonathan Rosenblum   Jeremy Kagan

TABLE OF CONTENTS

INTRODUCTION

WHY DO WE SUFFER?
A PERSONAL STATEMENT
BY RABBI KIRZNER

E ARE BEGINNING A SERIES OF DISCUSSIONS ABOUT suffering. Suffering is not an easy topic. On the theoretical level, it raises fundamental questions about our relationship with G-d. But the greatest challenge presented by our own suffering, or that of those whom we love, is not intellectual. It derives from the immediacy of the suffering. The pain, whether it be physical or psychological, strikes us directly. It affects the totality of our being, not just our ideas, and engenders powerful emotional responses that threaten to cut off discussion at its roots.

Suffering threatens that of which we are most conscious: our own existence. We invest all our energies
and abilities in giving direction and meaning to that
existence. And then suddenly, without warning, all
our hopes and aspirations are ripped away. We feel
insecure, cut loose from our moorings, and lonely. No
one else, we are sure, could possibly experience what
we are going through: the loss of our life as we previously knew it — a life so filled with hope for the future
and now so devoid of hope. We neither wish to confront our own suffering nor to discuss it with others,
for we know that, after all the words are spoken, the
pain will remain.

For a person of faith the loss is twofold. Just as his
life collapses around him, the relationship that has
until now been his greatest source of strength is called
into question more profoundly than ever before. All
his life he has been taught to believe in a G-d Who is
all-knowing, omnipotent, good and giving. Now he
feels abandoned by that G-d, or comes to doubt His
very existence. He fears that he will never again be
able to regain the warm, personal faith that characterized his relationship with G-d before things went so
hopelessly awry.

His thoughts are dominated by one question: How
could a G-d Who is good and just visit this suffering
upon me or allow it to happen? He is tormented by
doubts: How can I love You? How can I desire to be
close to You? How can I seek to mold my life in con-
formity with Your dictates, if You have abandoned me?

A person of faith requires faith. If he is unable to
sustain his relationship with G-d, the recognition of his

inability to do so provides no sense of release, no lessening of his anguish. The disappointment, the anger, the bewilderment, the loneliness all remain. Walking away from G-d offers no solution.

Though all pain is unique and private, the questions raised by that pain are common to all who suffer. The investigation of these issues therefore affords us one means of escaping our sense of being alone and abandoned.

Yet if the intellectual issues are age-old, the pain is immediate and personal. Our topic does not allow for a cold, theoretical investigation of the issues. Much more is at stake than just our ideas. Suffering tests how well we have integrated those ideas into the core of our beings. Faced with intense pain or life-threatening disease, all our pretenses fall away.

One who has not experienced intense suffering has neither the right nor the ability to discuss such an intensely personal topic. I'm not sure how much of my private life I want to share with you, but I will tell you that I am much better educated on this subject than I was two or three years ago. I do not approach the issue of suffering from an aloof, theoretical point of view, but as one who has wrestled, and continues to do so, with each one of these issues. I do not intend to merely address the theoretical questions, but to show you how they have been filtered through my own personal experiences.

The test of these explorations will be whether they leave us better able to cope with our suffering in positive, productive ways.

1

LAYING THE FOUNDATIONS

PRECISELY BECAUSE SUFFERING IS SO INTENSE, ANYONE caught in its throes longs for immediate answers to

The Limits of Reason

his questions and doubts. Unfortunately a hasty response to such emotionally and intellectually complex questions is inimical to the discovery of satisfying answers.

Before proceeding we must establish certain foundations. Most important, we must recognize from the outset the limitations of our understanding. If we seek an understanding that we cannot attain, we leave ourselves vulnerable to two possibilities, each disastrous in its own way. One possibility is frustration at our failure to find certitude and solace. The other is to mistake ignorance for knowledge, and to thereby deny ourselves the possibility of achieving true understanding.

Each of us likes to think of himself as an objective, dispassionate seeker of truth. And we would like to believe in our capacity to achieve objective understanding. In reality, however, our intellectual activities — especially our search for the meaning and purpose of life — are inevitably colored by our desires. There is no escaping our subjectivity.

The choice of topics to which we direct our mental energies are themselves a function of some pre-existing will or desire. Why does one person walk into a bookstore and gravitate to the section on Chinese cookbooks while another browses through the works of Greek philosophy? Only some pre-existing connection to one body of knowledge or another can explain the choice.

If subjectivity plays such a large role in the selection of information from which we forge our understanding, then it necessarily colors the results of those efforts as well. Different raw material inevitably yields different results.

Desire and will determine not only what information a person processes, but how it affects him. One can acquire factual knowledge without an affinity or interest in those facts, but information thus acquired will never change one's vision of himself or the world. That is what our Sages meant when they said, "A person does not learn Torah except from a place (i.e. on a topic) that his heart desires" (*Avodah Zarah* 19a).

The emphasis here is on the word learn. Without interest, education cannot take place. All successful educators are superior motivators, for without motivation teaching is impossible. Before we learn Torah for the first time every day, we recite a blessing. Within that blessing we include a short prayer that G-d should make the words of Torah sweet in our mouths (*Berachos* 11b). No other *mitzvah* is preceded by a similar petition: Before we put on *tefillin*, for instance, we do not ask G-d to please make the *mitzvah* enjoyable. But learning Torah is different. Without the sweetness, we cannot internalize the Torah.

Recognition of the correlation between our interest and our ability to absorb leads to some disturbing conclusions. Interest and desire are not only a means of internalizing knowledge; they are also a means of coloring it. If we pay attention only to those bits of information that interest us, then there is obviously a large subjective component to any intellectual investigation. Information that we perceive as beneficial to us takes on an exaggerated importance, and other information that threatens us in some way is filtered out.

The Torah makes this very point in the *Shema*, the basic affirmation of Jewish faith. In the third paragraph of the *Shema,* we are enjoined, "Do not go astray after your hearts ..." (*Numbers* 15:39). The Talmud interprets going astray after one's heart as referring to the pursuit of false ideologies and distorted beliefs about G-d (*Berachos* 12b).

Rabbi Elchonon Wasserman, one of the great leaders of European Jewry in the generation leading up to the Holocaust, asked: If the Torah warns against false ideologies and philosophies, why does it speak of the heart and not the mind? He answers: False beliefs are raised not so much by a defective intelligence as by a perverted heart. The heart is the seat of our desires and will, and those desires are the source of all distorted thinking.

To be sure, it is possible to reduce one's subjectivity. To the extent that a person gains control of his desires, he reduces the problem of bias. That is why purification of character is a precondition for greatness in Torah study.

Yet no matter how much we minimize our self-interest, the challenge raised by suffering confronts us with other inherent limitations. The ultimate answers to our questions necessarily depend on knowledge of G-d's ways and how He runs the world. As finite beings, however, we cannot know the ways of an infinite G-d. Our intellect cannot comprehend His. As Maimonides writes:

> His wisdom is not like the wisdom of the wisest of men, and the difference between Him and His creatures is not merely quantitative, but absolute.

Confronted with these barriers to intellectual understanding, what are we to do? Should we simply throw up our hands? Such a response is deeply unsatisfying. It is also un-Jewish.

Judaism, more than any other religion, demands rigorous, ongoing intellectual effort. We are not, of course, only thinking creatures, but as Jews and human beings, intellect is a crucial part of our essence. Any relationship with G-d that does not engage our intellect fails to move us at the deepest level of our beings. We must pursue our intellectual inquiries as far as we can, even as we remain mindful of our inherent limitations. We can neither abjure our intellect nor fully depend upon it.

Judaism does not view thought as the sole source of knowledge or truth. Nor does it limit truth to only those statements that can be verified in the same way as a logical proposition. Limiting our knowledge of the world to what can be philosophically or scientifically proven trivializes thought by confining it to a very narrow sphere. It equates the powerful, but limited, vision of science with the entirety of reality, and thereby excludes from the realm of legitimate inquiry all moral questions, as well as the nature of G-d and our relationship to Him.

G-d in His essence is unknowable, but that does not mean He does not exist. The totality of His ways is unfathomable, but that does not mean He has no ways.

Intellectual endeavor remains crucial, but it must be coupled with another element: trust. Trust is what we are left with when we have gone as far as we can towards intellectual understanding and have still not obtained satisfactory answers. Trust is the certainty that there is sense to G-d's ways even when we are denied access to those ways.

Relationship and Trust

MANY PEOPLE BELIEVE THAT HUMAN BEINGS CANNOT enter into a personal relationship with G-d. According to that view, such relations exist between people, but with respect to G-d there is only obligation: He commands, and we must obey.

That view is as destructive as it is prevalent. Those who think our connection to G-d is one of obligation only — I am commanded therefore I obey — tear the soul out of Judaism. The true Jewish view is just the opposite: Judaism enables finite Man to enter into a personal relationship with His Creator.

The purpose of doing *mitzvos* is not the commandments themselves. G-d does not command our performance because He needs something from us. Rather the *mitzvos* are the path to reach Him. Similarly, prayer is best understood as a one-way conversation with G-d, a conversation for the purpose of deepening the relationship.

All human relationships, though important in their own right, also teach us how to relate to G-d. King Solomon in *Song of Songs,* for example, uses the metaphor of the love of bride and groom to describe the ideal emotional bond between the Jewish people and G-d.

The strength of any relationship depends largely on the trust between the parties. A relationship between two people might originally be based on an enjoyment of one another's company. But unless each partner trusts the other, the potential for developing the relationship further is limited. For an intense emotional bond to develop between two people, they must be open with one another and not have to hide their true selves. Yet being open in this way entails risk and leaves one extremely vulnerable. No healthy person will open himself up to someone else unless he trusts the other not to misuse what he has revealed about himself.

Unless I believe that the other person genuinely seeks my benefit, and does not just view me as an object for the satisfaction of his or her needs, there can be no trust. If Leah doesn't trust Yaakov, then she is not relating to Yaakov as a person, she is relating to the qualities Yaakov displays when they are together. Leah is not really present in the relationship either. Her *enjoyment* derives from relating to Yaakov's displayed qualities, but she has not engaged or committed her *self*.

What we have said about human relationships is equally true of our relationship with G-d: The strength of that relationship depends on the degree of our trust that G-d seeks only our good. That trust can only develop, however, if we do not limit our relationship with G-d to that which we can fully comprehend.

If we only relate to G-d to the extent of our comprehension, we are not relating to G-d, but to our own intellect. If I accept G-d only to the extent that I fully understand Him, I am in reality worshipping myself; I have become the measure of all things. Such an attitude precludes a deep relationship with G-d. If we pull back every time understanding fails us, it is our understanding, not our selves, that has the relationship.

The *mitzvos* of the Torah are designed to teach us the necessity of going beyond our own finite understanding in our relationship with G-d. The Torah is filled with an entire class of commandments — *chukim* — that defy human comprehension.

G-d could have created us with the intellectual capacity to understand every *mitzvah*. Or He could have limited the Torah to only those *mitzvos* that we are capable of comprehending. But He did neither. Rather He gave us the *chukim* to introduce the element of trust into our relationship with him. We do not understand them. We observe them because we trust Him.

Trust in God, however, is not entirely the matter. If it were, this would be a very short book indeed. Just as trust must develop in the course of human relationships, so too must we develop trust in our relationship with God. Obviously, there must be some basis for trust in God, evidence of His goodness upon which that trust is founded.

Yet once that trust is established, it takes us past the limits of our rational understanding. The heart can go where the mind cannot. Sometimes we must be prepared to throw up our hands and say, "I don't understand why this is happening, but I know He is there." If we cannot do that, we doom ourselves to a very limited relationship with G-d.

EVERYTHING THAT WE HAVE SAID UNTIL NOW ABOUT THE necessity of trust in our relationship with G-d is im-

Trust and Suffering

portant in and of itself. But now we must explore its specific application to the issues raised by suffering.

Rabbi Moshe Chaim Luzzato (commonly referred to as *Ramchal* – the acrostic of his name), one of the greatest Jewish thinkers of the modern period, makes the following assertion: In dealing with issues of theodicy — the justice of God's running of the universe — we must content ourselves with the knowledge of the general rules. We can never understand the application of those rules to any particular case. Not only that. If we focus on the specific applications, we will not even grasp the general rules.

That insight has immediate application to us. We will, in the coming chapters, present a number of possible reasons why human beings suffer. Our classic sources list at least ten such reasons, and we shall examine each of them in detail. Each of these reasons will hopefully make sense on its own terms.

But even after we have enumerated all the possible reasons for suffering, many questions will be unanswered. Let us say, for instance, that one of the reasons for suffering is to enable the one suffering to realize previously untapped spiritual resources. In thinking about our own lives, we can all point to instances of adversity leading to growth. Yet that still leaves unanswered the question: Why is Reuven, not Shimon, singled out for growth? Everyone needs to grow spiritually. Why does G-d choose to further the spiritual growth of some and not others?

It is the latter sort of question, the *Ramchal* tells us, to which we can never know the answer. These are questions beyond the scope of human understanding. Answering them would require knowledge of the inner soul of each individual. It would require knowledge of factors that precede birth. And it would involve knowledge of the interplay between G-d's perfect judgment of each individual and His need to bring human history to its ultimate fulfillment. These calculations are beyond our capacity.

Thus the question that presses most urgently upon us in our suffering is precisely that which cannot be answered: Why me? Here we have moved beyond the realm of the mind to that of the heart. The mind can provide an outline of the general rules and a basis upon which trust becomes reasonable. But it cannot do more than that. At that point, the heart must take over. We have moved into the realm of trust.

Both mind and heart are crucial if we are to make peace with human suffering. But we must understand clearly at the outset the realm in which each works. If we attempt to substitute the mind for the heart in areas beyond its scope, we will reap only frustration.

We have to confront G-d, to the extent we can, on an intellectual level. But we must also approach Him on an emotional level, without blurring the boundaries between the two. Within each realm, we can yell, scream, and struggle as much as we want, but it will never help to employ the tools of one realm in the other.

We cannot shirk the questions posed by suffering. They cry out for answers. But we must know from the outset that our goal is to strike the delicate balance between understanding and trust. If we demand more of understanding than it can deliver, we invite frustration or disaster. By relying on the mind where the heart is required, we deprive ourselves of any true relationship with G-d.

The Torah provides several fascinating examples of individuals who, for all their greatness, failed to achieve the proper balance of head and heart, with disastrous consequences. The Torah devotes almost an entire *parashah* to Korach's rebellion against Moses. The Midrash informs us that Korach was upset at not being appointed as leader of the Levites, as he thought his due. As a consequence, he questioned Moses' motivations and ultimately the authenticity of the commandments transmitted by Moses to Israel. (Korach remains the classic example of how self-interest perverts understanding.)

Korach succeeded in attracting large numbers to his banner, including 250 heads of the Sanhedrin. Not only were Korach and all his followers killed, but his actions brought about a plague in which another 14,700 Jews lost their lives.

Korach, it seems, had a talent for amateur theatrics. According to the Midrash, he staged a skit designed to ridicule Moses. He declared that the *mitzvah* of *tzitzis,* which involves attaching eight strings, seven white and one *techeles* (azure), to each of the corners of four-cornered garments, did not originate with God (*Tanchuma, Korach* 2).

What Korach did was pure street theater. Korach gathered 250 men and dressed them in four-cornered garments that were totally azure. He presented them to Moses with great fanfare and demanded to know whether their garments still required *tzitzis.* Moses answered that they did, and Korach and his troupe began guffawing. "If one string of azure on each corner is sufficient for the entire garment," Korach challenged Moshe, "then why does a garment which is totally azure still require a string of azure?"

Korach crowed that he had proven that Moses made up the *mitzvah* of *tzitzis,* and if he made that up, who was to say that he had not made up all the other rules of the Torah as well?

Our sources describe Korach as a brilliant man. Even in a generation famed for its brilliance, Korach still stood out as a person of exceptional intelligence. Yet if we consider Korach's challenge, we wonder how his question could have convinced him or anyone else. True, the commandment of *tzitzis* requires that one string of azure be attached to each corner of a four-cornered garment. But the azure string did not hang by itself: there were also seven strings of white on each corner. How could Korach have supposed for a moment that a garment made up totally of azure was free of the obligation of the seven white strings on every corner?

To understand how Korach misled himself, we must first know something of the symbolism of the colors intertwined in the *tzitzis*. White represents that which is unknowable and beyond our comprehension. All the colors of the spectrum are contained in white, but not in a way that is visible. It signifies trust.

Azure, on the other hand, represents intellectual association and the investigative power of the mind. Azure reminds us of the color of the sea, and the sea in turn reminds us of the color of the sky, and the color of the sky, in turn, calls to mind the Divine Throne. These associations of the mind — from *tzitzis* through to the Divine Throne — make us aware of G-d.

What is the relationship of the two ideas symbolized in the *tzitzis?* The white threads form a spine around which the solitary azure thread is wound.

Without the base of white strings, there is nothing to hold up the blue strings. The message would seem to be that intellectual investigation must always be built upon a foundation of trust. Without that, the entire structure of *mitzvos*, which the *tzitzis* explicitly represent, collapses.

Korach understood the symbolism of the two colors. But he made one crucial error. He felt that the requirement of trust was limited to those of limited intellectual capacities. For those endowed with superior minds, he believed, everything can be derived intellectually — there is no need for trust in the relationship with G-d. Thus Korach could formulate a question predicated on the assumption that *tzitzis* require only an azure string.

What happened to Korach stands as an object lesson to all of us about the central role that trust must play in our relationship with Hashem. Without that element, Korach ended up denying the entirety of the Torah, even those parts capable of being grasped by the human intellect.

Nor was Korach the first to be misled about the importance of unaided intelligence. That tendency is as old as man himself. The first man, Adam, was created with such great spiritual potential that the angels mistook him for G-d Himself. He was placed in the Garden of Eden and provided with all the material bounty a person could desire. Only one thing was denied: he was not allowed to eat from the fruit of the Tree of Knowledge of Good and Evil. Yet even that one commandment proved too much for him. And he ate.

Rabbi Dessler, a great contemporary Jewish thinker, offers a fascinating account of Adam's failure, based on our Kabbalistic tradition. Adam felt that he was incapable of meaningful service of G-d. He perceived G-d's presence with such clarity that he could neither deny Him nor transgress His will. Adam reasoned that if he were to eat of the fruit and introduce the *yetzer hara* into himself, he would then be capable of a much deeper, more meaningful service of G-d — one based on choice and struggle with his *yetzer hara*.

There was only one problem with this line of reasoning. It was not what G-d had told him to do. Adam based his relationship with G-d exclusively on his own intellectual reasoning. He refused to obey the single commandment imposed upon him because he reasoned that he knew better than G-d what would constitute meaningful service.

By substituting his own understanding for that of G-d, he placed himself in the position of judging G-d. In essence, he worshipped himself, not G-d, though his ostensible goal was to deepen his Divine service. That is what the Talmud means when it accuses Adam of being a heretic (*Sanhedrin* 38b).

I hope no one will conclude that we have reached the end of the road as far as a discussion of suffering goes: There are no answers — only faith and trust. That is not what I'm trying to say. I am, however, seeking to establish the legitimacy of trust in our relationship with G-d.

Our task is to establish a balance between understanding and trust. We must emulate our ancestors who responded to Moses's offer of the Torah with the words, "We will do and we will understand" (*Exodus* 24:7). This statement is frequently described as the classic Jewish response. The commitment to do G-d's will precedes any understanding of His commandments.

But the Talmud does not stop there. Our ancestors were praised both for their commitment "to do" and "to understand" (*Shabbos* 88a). The desire to understand is also an essential aspect of our overall relationship with G-d. Trust must be the base, but we are nevertheless enjoined to use all our intellectual gifts so as to leave no part of ourselves out of our relationship with G-d.

2 PURPOSE: THE HEARTBEAT OF CREATION

N THE PRECEDING CHAPTER, WE ESTABLISHED THAT OUR efforts to reconcile the existence of suffering with our belief in a G-d Who is both omnipotent and benevolent must proceed simultaneously on two planes: one of intellectual understanding and the other of trust. From the outset, we must realize that definitive answers as to why one person suffers in a particular way are closed to us.

We can and will, however, identify reasons why Hashem allows suffering. Before doing so, however, we will first examine an alternative approach that has recently gained a great deal of prominence. Analyzing the faults of that approach will help clarify a coherent Jewish response to the problem.

THE OPPOSITE APPROACH MIGHT BE TERMED THAT OF randomness. According to this view, not everything that

A Failed Alternative

takes place in the world has a purpose or comes from G-d. Efforts to reconcile the existence of evil and suffering in the world with G-d's justice are a waste of time because they proceed from the false premise that everything that takes place in the world comes from G-d and has a purpose.

Harold Kushner, a Conservative rabbi, followed precisely such an approach in his best-selling book *Why Bad Things Happen to Good People*. Few "Jewish" books in recent decades have had a greater impact, and Kushner is regularly cited, in both the Jewish and non-Jewish media, as an expert on suffering and a variety of other ethical issues.

Kushner came to the topic of suffering through a terrible tragedy in his family: He and his wife lost a young son to a particularly perverse degenerative disease — premature aging syndrome. He has thus paid a heavy price for the right to talk about suffering. Though we shall be very critical of Kushner's conclusions, nothing we say should be seen as a personal criticism of him, or an attempt to in any way diminish the awful suffering he had to bear. It would be contemptible to pass judgment on another's experience of a tragedy of such magnitude.

If we are critical of Kushner's ideas, it is only because he has offered his views to the public as a consolation to those in pain and as an authentic Jewish response to the problem of suffering. As we shall see, they are neither.

While Kushner is in some sense a believer in G-d, his own faith was severely tested by the prolonged agony that he and his wife endured. He felt the need to construct a theory that would reconcile his tragedy with Judaism's belief in G-d's benevolence.

He concluded that to maintain his belief in G-d he must reject either G-d's benevolence or His omnipotence. He chose the latter course. G-d, in Kushner's view, created the world and provides the foundation of moral principle. But He cannot quite control the world He created. He hopes for our good and He sympathizes, as it were, with us in our pain, but He is powerless to do anything about it.

As to why a G-d Who had the power to create the entire universe in the first place would create one that He is powerless to control, Kushner basically shrugs his shoulders and contents himself with noting that the world is relatively good for most people most of the time. We might designate this theory as "randomness plus G-d."

Unable to understand why a good G-d would allow individuals to suffer, Kushner ends by neatly defining the question away. He cannot even conceive of the possibility of any understanding, and so concludes that we have no answers because there are no answers. Much of what happens is nothing more than random chance. Pain and tragedy are a necessary consequence of a world over which G-d does not exercise complete control.

The first thing that must be noted about this view is that it provides no solace whatsoever. Mrs. Kushner herself is on record as saying that she derived no comfort from her husband's theories. And that is not accidental. What good is it to know that G-d shares my pain if at the same time I am told that pain is utterly without meaning and purpose? Even if I cannot know the exact meaning of my personal suffering, I can still have faith that there is some purpose to that suffering. Kushner, however, denies the possibility of meaning, and with it any possibility of comfort.

There is no comparison between pain that is without purpose and meaning, and that which is purposeful. Childbirth is one of the most intensely painful experiences. Yet women willingly endure the agony of childbirth because they know that the end result is a child. A woman may not understand why pain must be the price for giving birth, but since it is, she accepts it.

The Jewish view of suffering, as we will learn later, is that it is part of a process of self-development — in effect a process of birth of the self. Though we would never choose intense suffering for ourselves, faith that it is part of a growth process can take away, if not the pain, at least some of its sting. Knowledge that the suffering has purpose and is leading somewhere offers me the strength to weather the crisis.

But if that suffering has no meaning, I am left all alone, a helpless victim of blind fate or randomness. Hearing that G-d feels my pain and laments my bad luck does not alleviate my sense of victimhood. Indeed, being told that my particular suffering somehow eluded G-d's notice until it was too late only exacerbates that sense of victimhood.

Compare the case of two laborers who both have their wages taken away. One has the money deducted from his paycheck and deposited in a pension fund. The other is mugged on the street. Both have lost their hard-earned money, but their reactions will be very different. For one the loss is only temporary; he is building for his future. The other, however, is bereft. He is a victim and nothing more. He cannot conceive of his mugging as leading to some future good.

If G-d Himself can find no rhyme or reason for my suffering, if there is no gain from my pain, how am I supposed to feel about it? How can I grow by viewing myself as the victim of chance? Far more than G-d's sympathy, I seek His assurance that whatever is happening to me is designed to lead somewhere and that I have not simply been abandoned to blind fate.

Kushner does argue that even if our suffering is random, it can be a means of personal growth and a means of deepening our sensitivities. But this is little solace. If G-d Himself judges the gain from our suffering not to be worth the price, how are we expected to feel?

Kushner's vision saps our emotional strength at times of suffering. But its effects go beyond just those instances of personal suffering and effect the entire sense of our place in the cosmos. What value are we supposed to attach to our life, if at any moment it can be cut off for no reason whatsoever? Without an answer to that question, Kushner's theory remains an emotional nightmare.

In the end, Kushner's vision fails to even achieve his original purpose: preserving G-d's benevolence. If G-d cannot prevent suffering, then neither can He direct Creation to bring about good. If He is not responsible for the bad, neither can He be credited with the good. If so, G-d's benevolence, which is central to both Jewish thought and that of Harold Kushner, is irretrievably lost.

Now, of course, because an idea is discomfiting and provides no comfort does not make it untrue. But Kushner's book not only fails to provide any comfort, it also is profoundly un-Jewish. Each of his main arguments runs counter to the traditional Jewish approach to the subject. They reflect accepted modern views far more closely than they do anything written in classical Jewish sources.

Morning and evening, Jews proclaim G-d's unity in the *Shema*. The *Shema*, with its assertion of G-d's absolute unity, constitutes the basic affirmation of Jewish faith. The Jewish belief in G-d's unity stands in stark contrast to paganism, based on a pantheon of competing gods, each with its own sphere of influence.

Kushner's view of the world is closer to Persian Manicheanism, in which the forces of Good and Evil are in constant struggle, than it is to traditional Judaism. He arrays a benevolent G-d, on one side, against the forces of randomness on the other. At best, his G-d is nothing more than a superman.

Kushner's G-d is a sovereign with very limited powers. Kushner has basically projected human limitation upon G-d. We have limits, so G-d has limits. Sometimes we are too busy to attend to all the details in our life, and G-d, too, sometimes loses track of the details.

All classical Jewish sources reject precisely such anthropomorphic projections of our human failings and limitations to G-d. The Jewish G-d is transcendental, completely different from us. We are physical beings, and as such subject to limitations. G-d is not a physical entity and knows no limitations. Maimonides describes the qualitative chasm between us and G-d:

> G-d is not physical and there is ab-
> solutely no comparison between Him
> and any of His creations. His existence
> is not like their existence; His life is not
> like that of any living being; His wis-
> dom is not like the wisdom of the
> wisest of men. The difference between
> Him and His creations is not merely
> quantitative, but absolute ...

Any similarity between Maimonides' G-d and Kushner's is purely coincidental. The G-d of Maimonides is the Creator and Source of all being — the uncreated One Who must exist, has always existed and will always exist. Since He necessitates all being, He can possess neither lack nor limitation.

Kushner's G-d, by contrast, is nothing more than an intellectual construct designed to save its author's belief in G-d's benevolence. His G-d is but a bit player in the heavenly hierarchy, playing a limited role in our existence, like the deities of Greek mythology.

By arguing that much of what happens is beyond G-d's control, Kushner effectively severs the connection between G-d and the world and thereby empties physical existence of all meaning. The events of our lives, as portrayed by Kushner, have no relationship to G-d.

Removing G-d, in this fashion, from an active role in the world and our lives is a complete distortion of all Jewish thought and living. Our faith as Jews does not end with an affirmation of belief in G-d's existence. G-d does not sit, as it were, in isolation in His heaven. Faith, for us, means that we are aware of the Divine Presence in every aspect of our world.

We are required, writes Rabbi Moshe Chaim Luzzato, to both "believe and know" that there is a G-d. This statement is hard to understand. If I know that there is a G-d, then belief is extraneous. The explanation is that knowing does not refer to empirical knowledge. Rather "knowing" refers to a process of relating our faith in G-d to everything we do. Knowing that there is a G-d means that our faith in Him must become inseparable from who we are and how we view the world.

Attaining this level is the work of a lifetime. Most of us are far from reaching it. We walk through life as if in a fog. Our faith remains theoretical at best. When we think about G-d, we forget the world. And when we think about the world, we forget G-d. No integration of G-d into our world takes place.

Occasionally, however, events intrude with such force that we are compelled to deal with our faith in the context of what is taking place in our lives.

Suffering is one such event. It challenges us to confront the ultimate questions of who we are and what is the significance of our lives. Suffering is a painful invitation to deepen our faith and make it a real part of our lives.

But that can only be done if we first recognize the physical world as G-d's creation and as an ongoing expression of His Will, which exists only as a medium for us to relate to G-d. By denying G-d's control over the events of our lives, however, Kushner denies meaning to those events and any possibility of using them to deepen our relationship with G-d.

In the face of acute suffering, he would strengthen the chasm between G-d and the world, and thus ensures that G-d remains irrelevant to our lives — an intellectual concept to be retrieved intermittently. He thus denies us any possibility of solace through a deepened relationship with G-d.

Having seen why a philosophy of randomness undermines rather than strengthens our faith in moments of crisis, let us now examine the traditional Jewish view, which is the very antithesis of Kushner's: the belief that everything that happens in the world has a purpose.

JUDAISM BEGINS WITH THE BELIEF IN A CREATOR OF THE entire universe. The history of our people commences with Avraham's question, "Who created the world?" (cf. *Bereishis Rabbah* 39:1). That question led him to the recognition of G-d as the Creator.

Purpose and Providence

G-d existed prior to Creation, and that Creation remains dependent upon Him. Creation came into being as an expression of His will and is dependent on Him; it continues to exist only by virtue of a continued infusion of His creative energy. This is stated in the first of the Thirteen Principles of Faith based on Maimonides: "The Creator, Blessed is His Name, creates and guides all creatures, and He alone created, creates, and will create everything."

Now, if G-d created the world and continues to sustain it, He must have had some purpose. Intelligent beings do not act without some purpose, and certainly the Supreme Intelligence must be assumed to act in a purposeful fashion. Prior to Creation, G-d was complete unto Himself. He had no need for the world, for He lacked nothing. Indeed, as the Kabbalists put it, He had to make room for the world, as it were, through an act of voluntary contraction.

Creation, then, has a goal. A crucial corollary to this belief is: G-d created the world in such a way as to ensure that it would eventually reach the goal for which He intended it. No one invests his time and energy for no reason. And neither did G-d.

True, we often start projects with great expectations and subsequently find ourselves incapable of realizing our hopes for one reason or another. But we err if we project our own limitations onto G-d. We are incapable of accurately foreseeing all the intervening events that may prevent us from realizing our goal, and our abilities may prove unequal to our aspirations.

God, however, suffers no such limitations. First, it is another one of our fundamental beliefs that G-d has absolute foreknowledge of everything that will ever happen. Thus it is absurd to suggest that He created a world in which His very purpose in creating it could not be realized.

Furthermore, we, as human beings, try to manipulate the pre-existing materials of the world to achieve our purposes. But G-d did not create the world from pre-existing material. He is the source of all the raw material from which the world is formed. He imbued everything with its potential. It is impossible to imagine those raw materials acting in a manner contrary to G-d's will. Moreover, G-d exercises a constant veto power over the direction in which His creation is headed. Nothing continues to exist except because of His sustaining power.

These points are crucial. Though we believe that G-d created the universe, we are generally oblivious to the implications of our belief. We continue to relate to G-d as if He too were a part of Creation — a bigger and stronger part, to be sure, but a part nevertheless — rather than as the independent Creator of all that exists. Because of this laziness of thought, we project our own limitations onto G-d and cannot conceive of Him as capable of overseeing every aspect of Creation.

But when we make ourselves aware of G-d's true relationship to Creation, we realize that just as G-d created the world with a purpose so He has the capability to provide whatever guidance is required to accomplish that goal. That ability is Divine Providence.

Divine Providence posits that not only did G-d create the world for a specific purpose — a purpose which remains constant for all time — but that He maintains a relationship with His Creation sufficient to ensure that those purposes are ultimately achieved.

The traditional Jewish belief in Divine Providence is thus the antithesis of the view that there is a realm in which randomness governs. A belief in randomness cannot be reconciled with Divine Providence.

One of the crucial corollaries to the belief in Divine Providence is that not only does Creation as a whole have a particular purpose, but so does every single aspect of that Creation. Among those aspects of the created world are our lives. And just as G-d directs the totality of Creation towards its ultimate goal, so does He direct our lives in such a way as to make it possible for us to fulfill our purpose.

This realization has profound implications for our entire self-perception. For if our lives have purpose, and if G-d is continually overseeing our lives to ensure that we retain the possibility of fulfilling our purpose, it is impossible that some totally random event could knock us out of the ballpark in such a way as to prevent us from reaching the goal for which we were destined.

Divine Providence guarantees that we are provided with the necessary environment to accomplish our specific tasks. Nothing can destroy that capability.

Divine Providence requires that I think to myself, "I was brought into the world for a reason. G-d invested in me, and every moment that I am breathing, it is only because He still has hope that I will accomplish the tasks for which I was created." That view cannot be reconciled with the view that my life may be taken away from me at any moment for no reason whatsoever, through the workings of chance.

Providence endows my life with significance. Randomness takes this away. How much value can there be to life that can be snatched away at any moment for no reason?

HAROLD KUSHNER ASKS HOW G-D CAN BE GOOD IF OUR lives are not. Based on his perception of the quality of our lives, he proceeds to judge G-d and finds Him wanting — too wanting, in fact, to believe that He has anything to do with the quality of our lives.

Good and Bad

Judging G-d is a dangerous game, for it means employing the standards of our finite intelligence to judge His infinite intelligence. Yet if we ask the question of why certain things are happening to us, not to judge G-d, but to clarify the nature of our relationship, the question is not only legitimate but essential. A failure to ask the question would itself betray a lack of trust in G-d, and imply that He has no connection to what happens to us. A faith too timid to confront these questions cannot anchor our sense of the deeper reality underlying the sensory world.

Now, it must be clear that Kushner's question presupposes a clearcut standard by which to evaluate the quality of our lives. But Kushner has not thought rigorously about this problem. He entitled his book *Why Bad Things Happen to Good People*. But, if we look at his use of the terms "good" and "bad," it would appear that they are not being used consistently.

Kushner uses "good" and "bad" as synonyms for pleasant and unpleasant. A good life is a pleasant one in his view. As applied to people, he uses "good" to mean affable and pleasant. Classical Jewish thought, however, deals with the issue of the suffering of the "righteous" — those who lead their lives consonant with G-d's Will.

The use of "good" and "bad" as synonyms for "pleasant" and "unpleasant" is not very satisfactory. Much that is pleasant nevertheless has very negative consequences, and that which is unpleasant can be very positive.

Smoking may be pleasant, but it kills. Many medicines are bitter — some, like those used in chemotherapy, extremely so — yet they can save lives.

In place of pleasant and unpleasant, Jewish thought insists on another standard of evaluation: purposeful and not purposeful. Nothing is more essential to our status as human beings than the pursuit of meaning in our lives. That quest grows from the fact that each of us is made up of a body that is physical, and which will eventually cease to exist, and a soul that is infinite.

The soul craves connection to the Infinite from which it came; a connection to something beyond the confines of the body and physical existence. That connection can only make sense in the context of a structure of meaning anchored outside the self. The search for such a structure in itself reflects the need of the soul for a connection to the Infinite.

The greatest pain that a human being can experience is the sense that the events of his or her life lack any purpose and are not directed towards any goal. Purpose is an essential aspect of all intelligent activity, and as intelligent beings the failure to find any purpose in our lives undermines our entire sense of self. Where a sense of purpose exists, we are able to endure incredible suffering, for that suffering does not violate the awareness of our essential humanity. On the other hand, where it is absent, there is only a sense of inner emptiness, no matter how many pleasurable sensations one experiences.

Once purpose becomes the yardstick by which we evaluate our lives, we are forced to identify the purpose of our lives. Since the quest for meaning reflects the quest of our souls for connection with the Infinite, that meaning or purpose must exist outside of ourselves. This quest for meaning inevitably leads us to ask: Why did G-d create us?

WHY DID G-D CREATE THE WORLD? WHAT DID HE SEEK TO accomplish? Obviously He needed nothing from the

The Purpose of Creation

Creation since He is by definition complete and perfect unto Himself. "Need" implies that one lacks something, and G-d could not have lacked anything He Himself created.

To fully understand God's purpose would require knowledge of G-d prior to His interaction with His Creation — i.e., knowledge of His essence, not just how He expresses Himself in human history — and that is beyond the reach of human understanding. We can know nothing of G-d prior to Creation.

We must therefore turn to the Torah, as we do for all knowledge that is both essential and beyond our capacity to derive by ourselves. And when we look into the Torah, we find that G-d created the world out of a desire to give. As King David says in Psalms, "… a world which manifests Your loving kindness, You did build" (*Psalms* 89:3). Giving requires a receiver. So G-d created human beings to be the recipients of His bounty.

G-d's giving bears no comparison to our giving. When we reach into our pocket to give charity to a poor individual, for instance, we do so, in part, to relieve a feeling of discomfort caused by the sight of a fellow human being in need. Prior to Creation, however, there was nothing outside of G-d, nothing to arouse feelings of pity. Thus His desire to give was completely generated from within Himself. It was an expression of His overflowing goodness.

We human beings may give out of a variety of motivations, some good and some bad. Giving in order to aggrandize oneself at the expense of another or to manipulate another by fostering dependence fall into the latter category. Such giving is in reality taking. But since G-d needs nothing, His giving is never motivated by a desire to take. It is of necessity without taint of self-interest and solely for the benefit of the recipient.

As a perfect giver, G-d wants to give the perfect gift. That gift is the possibility of a connection with G-d Himself, for He Himself is the source of all true good.

Therefore G-d created a being who is capable of cleaving to Him.

G-d could give endlessly, but that would not be for our ultimate good as recipients. Indeed, it would ultimately destroy the possibility of giving at all. Were G-d's goodness to flow automatically to us, we would cease to be independent beings and become mere extensions of Him. The first condition of giving — the existence of an entity distinct from the giver — would be destroyed.

True giving, then, is predicated on the existence of the human self. Free gifts undermine our sense of self. When we receive something without earning it or being worthy of it, we disappear in the awareness of our total dependence upon the giver. Anyone who has received an undeserved gift recognizes this. As much as we might enjoy the gift itself, we experience an embarrassment that is akin to a little death of self.

We enjoy that which is the product of our efforts far more than any gift. A person prefers one *kav* (a measure of 2.2 liters) of his own produce to nine *kav* of others, say our Sages (*Bava Metzia* 38a) precisely because that *kav* represents the fruits of his own efforts. Similarly, a teenager who works for a year to buy an old Ford, which he himself then keeps running smoothly, derives more pleasure from it than a peer who borrows his father's BMW whenever he wants. It makes no difference that the BMW is the better car, for it represents nothing of his own efforts.

We prefer what we earn over what is given to us because the desire to earn reflects the underlying nature of reality. Creation, as an expression of G-d's giving, is only comprehensible in the context of our capacity to earn His bounty, for only that capacity makes us independent recipients.

Now we can understand why G-d does not simply give us everything that we want, unrelated to our worthiness to receive. To do so would not be to our benefit, for we would lose our ability to enter into a relationship with G-d. And giving which is not for our good would itself not be consistent with G-d's desire to give.

Note that this description of G-d's giving also imposes obligations upon us. For if the sole purpose of Creation is only that G-d be able to give, then we have a reciprocal obligation to make ourselves the worthy recipients of His bounty. Our failure to do so stymies the purpose of Creation itself.

This description of G-d's purpose provides us with an entirely new measuring stick to evaluate our lives. No longer will we judge our lives in terms of pleasure and pain, for pleasure and pain do not by themselves provide meaning to life. True, we still hope that our lives will be pleasurable, but even very great pain need not raise fundamental questions about G-d's goodness. For even great pain may be judged good if it prepares us for our purpose in life, which is to enter into a relationship with God. From this standpoint, our maturity as Jews is measured by the degree to which we define ourselves, not in terms of our immediate circumstances, but in terms of our ultimate goal of becoming worthy of receiving from G-d.

APPLYING THE STANDARD OF PURPOSE TO JUDGE THE EVENTS
of our lives dramatically alters our perspective on the

Deserving and Undeserving

challenge that suffering poses to faith. We typically perceive human suffering as unjust, and thus a contradiction to our belief in a just G-d. Purpose, however, broadens our frame of reference in such a way that the question disappears.

Viewing life through the perspective of purpose forces us to ask: Is my pain bringing me closer to my ultimate goal in life? To answer that question requires a good deal more information than simply evaluating the degree of present suffering. The relevant time frame now includes the future. In order to justify G-d's ways, we are no longer limited to evaluating present experiences as responses to past actions; our present experiences are also opportunities for future growth. A particular experience, for instance, may offer such potential for growth as to far outweigh the immediate pain.

We are not prophets, and so we cannot know the future. But all of us know from personal experience that what appears to us today as a devastating setback may turn out to be the source of our greatest blessing. Certainly we know many who have reached their fullest potential as human beings only in the face of adversity.

Judgments based on the narrow lens of the present must be tempered by the knowledge that we are observing only a small fraction of the relevant tableau. The present pain threatens to overwhelm all else and obscure the magnitude of the reward that potentially awaits us. That reward, as we shall see in the next chapter, is far greater than any pleasure in this world. But without awareness of its existence, we lack the tools to properly assess whether our present suffering is "worth it."

Asking ourselves whether present suffering is purposeful — i.e., is it bringing us closer to G-d — not only helps us reevaluate suffering that seems undeserved, but also that which may appear to us to be deserved. If someone does something wrong, and subsequently something bad happens to him or her, the natural tendency is to chalk up the latter event as some form of punishment from G-d — the just desserts of his action, as it were.

Yet there is no such concept in the Torah of G-d meting out punishment in this world. G-d never simply inflicts pain as punishment, for such punishment has nothing to do with His purpose in creating the world. His purpose was to give. What we term "deserved suffering" from our perspective is not designed to punish, but rather to make it possible for G-d to give to the person thus afflicted, either by purging him of impurities caused by his sins or by directing him back to the correct path. What we perceive as "punishments" are pathways to enable man to come closer to G-d.

WE MIGHT STILL ASK: IF G-D CREATED THE WORLD IN ORDER to give, why must He be the one to define the nature of the gift? If we are content with the immediate pleasures of this world, why can't G-d just give us these? Why must we

Choosing Life

accept pain and suffering as prods to return us to a path leading to closeness to G-d? After all, true giving is for the benefit of the recipient, not the one giving. Why can't we choose the good we want to receive? Why must our lives run according to His standard?

From what we have already said, the answer to these questions should be apparent. Man's search for meaning, as described above, is the quest of a soul seeking to break free of the constraints of the finite body to fulfill a purpose that has been determined outside of itself. That external standard is established by G-d, the Infinite Other, Who stands completely independent of us.

G-d imbued the universe with purpose. He created us in order to make possible the most perfect gift, a relationship with Him. Anything that does not facilitate that relationship is by definition devoid of meaning and deters us from the purpose for which we were created.

The above questions betray a fundamental misunderstanding of the nature of our existence. They start with the attitude that having been brought into existence against our will, we nevertheless possess our lives once here. We, not G-d, should determine the conditions of our further existence.

The Jewish view, however, is the opposite. Our existence requires G-d's continual support every moment. Were He to cease to sustain us for even one instant, we would vanish completely. And He only continues to support our existence as a vehicle for reaching the goals for which we were brought into this world in the first place.

G-d wants us to choose life over death. If we choose not to draw close to Him, we are effectively choosing death. By pursuing the pleasures of the world we cut ourselves off from Him.

Because of His desire to give, G-d cannot simply let us kill ourselves (though we may eventually succeed). Imagine a father who gives his college-bound son a credit card. Rather than using the credit card for school expenses, the son uses the credit card for drugs and fast cars. One day the father receives news that his son overdosed in his new sports car. Needless to say he immediately cancels his son's credit card. The father did not give his son a credit card to facilitate his self-destruction, and will show no sympathy to his son's protestations that he is entitled to use the credit card as he wishes.

Similarly, G-d does everything in His power to keep us from destroying ourselves, which is what we do when we render ourselves unfit to receive His bounty.

3 THE SOUL PERSPECTIVE

N THE PREVIOUS CHAPTER, WE DISCUSSED HOW A CHANGE OF focus can dramatically alter our approach to the topic of suffering. By changing our question from, "Am I enjoying this experience or not?" to "Is there any purpose to what I am experiencing?" we may come to a very different evaluation of events that we previously labeled unambiguously bad.

Similarly, most of us tend to evaluate the events of our lives within a very narrow time frame. We think, "How does this affect me now?" Yet as we grow older, most of us can point to examples of events that seemed like overwhelming tragedies at the time that turned out to be the source of our greatest blessing. To fully evaluate suffering we must not only expand our time frame from the past to the immediate present, we must expand it to include the World to Come as well.

Expanding our frame of reference to include the World to Come shifts our focus from our bodies to our souls. Most of us tend to judge what is happening to us by its effect on our physical existence. But that is a very constricted perspective. To understand ourselves we must also consider the impact of events on our soul. That requires a perspective that includes the World to Come.

MERE MENTION OF THE AFTERLIFE PROBABLY SETS ALARM bells ringing in most people's heads. "Oh, no; the

A Brief Comment on the World to Come

rabbi is going to explain away all the problems by telling us not to worry — no matter how bad things are in this world you will be fully compensated in the World to Come."

Many people are instinctively suspicious of "solutions" to problems that depend on the afterlife since none of us have any direct experience of that afterlife. Such solutions strike us as evasive.

That suspicion is well-founded — at least as the afterlife is usually presented. Frequently the World to Come is described as if it were a lollipop awarded to those who shoulder their suffering in this world without complaint. The attitude expressed is: "Life may be tough, but it does not really count anyway; the important stuff is later, and we'll make it up to you then. Just be patient."

Not surprisingly, many conclude that discussions of the afterlife are mere distractions from our proper task of living this life properly. Among non-observant Jews, it is widely believed that Judaism has no concept of an afterlife at all. They contrast Judaism to Christianity as a "this-worldly" religion. Judaism, they claim, values only deeds; Christianity emphasizes faith. Such descriptions betray a striking lack of knowledge of classical Jewish sources, which are filled with discussions of the World to Come.

The rejection of belief in the afterlife by contemporary Jews is based on a profound misunderstanding of the Jewish concept of the World to Come. In Judaism, the afterlife is not something completely removed from, and independent of, this world. Rather it is the culmination of life in this world.

We create our own eternity through our actions in this world. Our World to Come is the direct product of what we make of ourselves in this world. Viewed in this way, the concept of the afterlife does not empty our actions in this world of significance. Rather it enhances their importance by placing those actions in a more profound context. Knowledge of the end to which our lives are heading provides us with a context to judge the various steps along the way.

The Soul Breath of the Divine

IN THE PRECEDING CHAPTER, WE ARGUED THAT G-D CREATED the world in order to give. The greatest gift that G-d can give man is a relationship with Him. But how can finite man come close to an infinite G-d?

What possible basis exists for a shared relationship? How can man partake of the infinity of G-d?

We are forced to the conclusion that man contains within himself something infinite as well. That is what we mean when we say that man was created in the Divine Image. G-d took of Himself in order to create man. That part of man that comes from G-d Himself we call the soul — the divine spark from above.

We can draw close to G-d precisely because of that divine spark. Because of it man is not wholly foreign to G-d; he contains within himself something of G-d's essence and is therefore capable of cleaving to G-d.

The Torah describes the process by which G-d invested man with that part from Himself as a process of blowing into man's nostrils: "He blew into his nostrils the breath of life" (*Genesis* 2:7). *Va'yipach*, the Hebrew verb employed to describe this blowing, denotes a deep blowing that draws on all the reserves of the lungs. When a person blows in this way, he utilizes his full strength to harness the very breath upon which his life depends. This is alluded to in the rabbinic statement, "He Who blew, blew from Himself," meaning from His "inner essence," as it were. Thus G-d invested of His essence in the creation of man.

The imparting of a G-dly soul into man did not merely add another dimension to man's being. It formed the basis of his humanity. Without the soul, he might have been ambulatory and possessed the same life-force as any animal but he would not have been man.

Every Rosh Hashanah, we experience again at a subconscious level that moment when G-d blew into our nostrils and invested us with a soul. The shofar blasts require the one blowing the shofar to draw upon the full capacity of his lungs. The powerful exhaling necessary to extract a sound from the shofar imitates the deep blowing with which G-d endowed Adam with a soul. The haunting blasts of the shofar awaken a primordial memory of the moment when the *neshamah* (soul) entered the body.

The experience of coming into being can be compared to a deep-sea diver coming to the surface after the air in his lungs has been exhausted. As he approaches the surface, he can think of nothing else other than the absolute necessity to refill his lungs with oxygen. Awareness of the absolute need for air fills him with terror, until that climactic moment when he breaks the surface and can again drink in life-giving air in desperate gasps.

Similarly, as our soul entered our body, we began to awaken to self-consciousness. We became aware of our absolute need for our soul before that soul was fully ours. Over time, the experiences of physical existence dim the memory of that moment when we recognized our absolute dependence on our soul. The shofar rekindles within us the memory of that moment. The memory evoked is the source of the shofar's mystical power.

WHAT FOLLOWS FROM THIS PICTURE OF THE SOUL AS THE defining element of our humanity? Man is not essen-

Man as a Spiritual Being

tially a physical being to whom G-d has, in His kindness, added a pinch of spiritual consciousness. No, the body without the soul is like the diver whose lungs have been depleted. Unless he receives an immediate infusion of oxygen, he will die.

King David captures the relationship of the soul to the body in *Psalms* when he proclaims five times, *"Barchi nafshi es Hashem,* My soul, praise Hashem" (*Psalms* 103:1,2, 22, 104:1, 35). The experiences of his life revealed to David *HaMelech* five parallels between G-d's relationship to the world and the soul's relationship to the body. In the words *barchi nafshi,* the Talmud finds an allusion to the idea, "Let the one who has these five characteristics come and praise the One Who has these five characteristics" (*Berachos* 10a).

The Talmud then goes on to list five parallels between the relationship of the soul to the body and G-d's relationship to the world.

"Just as G-d sustains the whole world, so the soul sustains the body," is one such parallel. Though G-d lacks any physical attributes and yet still sustains the entire physical world, so too the soul, which lacks any physical attributes, sustains the body. Were G-d to cease sustaining the world for the most fleeting instant, the entire physical world would disappear. And similarly, a human being cannot live without being nurtured by his or her soul. Thus the soul is primary, for it is the soul that gives life to the body and not vice versa.

According to King David, without the spiritual force of the soul, man cannot exist at all. To describe the soul in any other way is to reduce man to the status of an animal with a bit of a spiritual flair. Our soul is not the cherry on top of a chocolate sundae; it is our essence.

The question might be asked: Doesn't the existence of the entire animal kingdom — insects, birds, fish, mammals — prove that it is possible to sustain life without any connection to the soul we have been describing? The answer to that question is that Judaism views man as qualitatively distinct from every other created being. He is not just a smarter, more sophisticated animal. While all other species possess a life-force and physical existence without a richness of spiritual energy, not so man. Man cannot be conceived apart from his spiritual energy.

That is not to say that the body is insignificant. But it is the soul that is primary and the body which is secondary. Though we are comprised of body and soul, the body was created to serve the needs of the soul and not the other way around.

While the root and source of our self is the soul, it is through the body that the soul expresses itself. The body provides the context within which we exercise our free will and thus express the potential of our souls. Without the challenges into which our body thrusts us, the soul would remain forever in potential, unrealized.

WHAT HAPPENS WHEN THE BODY STOPS FUNCTIONING AND WE die? Without the body to provide the challenges of life,

What Happens When We Die?

the soul can no longer grow. The stage of the development of the soul and the realization of its potential is over.

The Soul Perspective / 45

But while the body ceases to be alive and decom-poses, the soul does not. Death marks the end of the opportunity for change in the soul, but it does not effect any change in the soul itself. Whatever capaci-ty of the soul we developed in our lives remains intact even after bodily death. That is the Jewish conception of the afterlife.

Our Sages found many metaphors in the physical world for the new stage ushered in by death. In truth, metaphor is not really the right term, for it suggests a chance relationship between the *mashal* and *nimshal,* between the metaphor and what it represents. And there is nothing accidental about the relationship of physical processes to spiritual ideas. The physical world reflects a deeper spiritual reality, or more pre-cisely, it is the physical expression of a particular spir-itual reality. We can therefore gain access to deeper spiritual truths through the study of physical reality.

For example, *Eretz Yisrael* (the Land of Israel) relies entirely on rainfall for its supply of water, unlike Egypt which is irrigated by the Nile. The rain in *Eretz Yisrael* is intermittent and unreliable, as opposed to the constant flow of the Nile. That difference between *Eretz Yisrael* and Egypt is a direct consequence of the former's designation as the designated Land of the Jewish people. Our dependence on rain in *Eretz Yisrael* ensures that we will always turn to G-d in prayer, and reflects the special level of Divine Providence that governs the Land.

Our Sages view death not as an end, but as a new birth. And they found many allusions to this process in the physical world. Take the course by which a seed becomes a new plant. The farmer labors hard to produce that seed, and yet no sooner has he obtained it, than he plants it in the ground. There the shell around the kernel decays. Decomposition — the "death" of the body around the seed — must take place for a new plant to come forth. The essence of the seed, its inner kernel, is preserved, but it too must disappear in its present form before it can give birth to the ultimate goal — a shoot growing into a plant. The spiritual concept hinted at by this process is that sometimes the outer shell must "die" so that the inner essence can be expressed.

Spring, too, serves as a metaphor for the new birth that we call the afterlife. For months, it is dark and gloomy; everything is frozen or sleeping. Suddenly, one day it begins to thaw. Soon the world fills with blossoming flowers and chirping birds. What had seemed like death turns out to have been a period of transition during which the world was preparing for a spurt of new life.

To sensitize us to what we witness, our Sages initiated a special blessing to be recited on first seeing the fruit trees in bloom: "Blessed are You, Hashem, our G-d, King of the universe, Who left nothing lacking in His universe, and created in it goodly creatures and goodly trees, to bring pleasure to mankind."

Why are we elevated by the sight of new blossoms? Because the new blossoming after the death of winter enables us to relate to the spiritual concept of the rebirth of the soul after death. Only after shedding the external husk of its body does the soul realize its full potential.

G-d could have created the world with a uniform climate year-round, but He chose instead to create the seasons, with their cycle of death and renewal, so that we would know that such a cycle exists at a deeper level as well.

With this new perspective on death, we are prepared to confront our own mortality. The terror that death holds for most people is its finality. One day we are vibrant and producing, and then death arrives and all comes to an abrupt halt. That is how it appears to us.

G-d wants us to know that it is not so. We have been given eternal life. The death of our body involves nothing more than taking off one suit of clothes and putting on another. Viewed in this way, we need not fear death. But we must still understand our task in this world and its relationship to the reward of the World to Come.

WHEN WE DESCRIBE OUR SOUL AS OUR ESSENTIAL SELF, WE mean, among other things, that since it is eternal it is of far greater worth than the body

The Soul as the Ultimate Recipient of G-d s Reward

which is transitory. But we mean something else as well. We have already described how the yardstick for evaluating the events of our lives is their relationship to G-d's purpose in creating us, which is to be the recipients of His goodness.

How is that goodness received? What part of us is capable of entering into a relationship with G-d? Obviously it is the soul.

We receive G-d's goodness through cleaving to Him. That cleaving to God can only take place if man and G-d share something in common. That common element cannot be the body. G-d is infinite; our bodies finite. G-d is eternal; our bodies live for but a few decades.

Rather that common element lies in man's soul — a breath of G-d Himself. The soul is not bound by the limitations of the physical world and time. Only it can receive G-d's ultimate goodness, which is awareness of Him.

Thus the purpose of life must be evaluated in terms of our soul. The measure of events in this world is the opportunity they provide to bring out the capacities of the soul. The capacity of the soul determines how much of G-d's goodness it will absorb in the World to Come.

King David made this point when he praised G-d through the medium of his soul — *borchi nafshi*. It is our souls that can praise G-d because it is through our souls alone that we are capable of a relationship with Him.

ALL OF THIS IS VERY FRIGHTENING. MOST OF US ARE FAR more aware of our bodies than we are of our souls —

Why the Soul Perspective is so Hard to Attain

at least most of the time. And so when we are told that our essence is our soul, and that the pleasures of the body are at best a means to a higher purpose, we feel threatened. Our identity is wrapped up in our physical existence. To question the significance of our physical existence calls our entire sense of self into question.

Living with this "soul perspective" is hard, very hard. It goes against the most concrete thing we possess, the evidence of our senses. We know with absolute clarity that we exist physically. When we look in the mirror we see our bodies, and we think, "This is me." When we eat, we taste the food and feel the satisfaction of being full. An awareness of ourselves as physical beings does not need to be cultivated; it is automatic.

By contrast, awareness of ourselves as possessing a divine soul must be cultivated. Many never achieve this consciousness at all. And this raises a question: If our soul is the essence of our humanity, why did G-d make it so difficult to attain an awareness of that soul and so easy to focus on our immediate, sensory existence?

Another question will help us answer the first. As we have said, our souls come directly from G-d; they are divine. But if they are directly from G-d, in what sense are they ours? The answer is that we are given a soul in an undeveloped state, and it is our task to develop that soul through its contact with the world. We do not create our souls, but we do create a relationship with the soul, and in doing so we create *ourselves* as expressions of our soul.

Only by struggling to define ourselves in terms of the soul do we gain possession of our souls. G-d places many barriers in our path. In the course of overcoming these barriers, we develop our souls and come to possess them as our own.

G-d created us in such a way that our natural inclination is to remain unconscious of our souls and focus on our bodies. He did not do so because the body is more essential than the soul. Quite the opposite. G-d obscured our awareness of the soul, for only by overcoming the barriers placed in our path does the soul become something earned and thus our own.

By choosing to ignore that which is most evident to our senses, we struggle for our souls. That struggle is not just the discovery of our true selves but the creation of that self. Through that struggle, the unformed soul, like an unminted blank coin, receives the impression of a personality and a particular self.

WHILE OUR AWARENESS OF OURSELVES AS PHYSICAL BEINGS tends to overwhelm the consciousness of our spiritual essence, we are not without tools

Learning to Think of Ourselves as Spiritual Beings

for gaining consciousness of our souls. Chief among those tools is reflection.

For the most part, physical pleasures draw us because they tend to be instantaneous and easily achieved. Stimulate the appropriate nerve endings and the reward is immediate. Less noticed, however, is that physical pleasures are also very fleeting. No matter how powerful the physical experience, it leaves no lasting imprint. Memory itself is inadequate to conjure up even the most powerful physical pleasures. Such pleasures cannot outlive the body, for they have no connection to non-physical existence. When the body declines and dies everything connected with it ends as well.

Most of us to some degree or another also sense that physical pleasures are qualitatively different from spiritual pleasures. Even in our speech, when we describe someone as shallow, we mean that he has no access to pleasures beyond the physical. No matter how much physical pleasure a person achieves, there usually comes a point in life in which he recognizes that the single-minded pursuit of such pleasures is inherently degrading, and that the cost of achieving those pleasures is loss of human dignity.

As those who devote themselves to physical pleasure age and their capacity for physical pleasure diminishes, life itself often comes to seem worthless in their eyes. By contrast, one whose pleasures have always been of a more spiritual nature suffers no decrease in his enjoyment of life.

A roller coaster ride momentarily overwhelms us in a way that spiritual joys rarely do. Yet a life lived in pursuit of such moments of excitement is of necessity one lived in the debit column; the moments of excitement are inevitably outnumbered by those in between.

The joy of watching your child taking his first step is less overwhelming than a roller coaster ride, but we instinctively recognize that it touches a deeper, more fundamental aspect of our being. The satisfaction penetrates to a much deeper part of our self.

On the roller coaster we are acutely aware of the contrast between what we are experiencing and all the humdrum moments of our life. Even as we experience pleasure, we are conscious of the fact that most of our life is not like this. But when we observe our child take his or her first tentative steps, we experience a certain peace, a sense of a connection to something beyond our physical bodies. The intense joy of the moment makes us aware of something that is always there, something constant. Rather than depressing us by highlighting a contrast to our normal everyday existence, as does the roller coaster ride, moments of intense joy, like watching a child's first step, heighten our sense of well-being.

The satisfaction that comes through development of our inner selves touches the deepest recesses of our being. The pleasure experienced is not momentary; we feel that what we have gained will last for eternity. Unlike the body, the soul lives forever. Every realization of the potential of our soul represents an eternal gain. The depth of the experience reflects its eternal consequences.

We are constantly confronted with a choice of pursuing the pleasures of the body or those of the soul. Let us think of the choice as a business investment. If we had to choose between renting a home or purchasing the same home by taking out a mortgage entailing payments equal to the rent, we would obviously prefer the mortgage. When the mortgage payments are all made, we will own the home unencumbered. But if we just pay rent all those years, we shall have nothing left to show for our expenditures.

When we focus on physical pleasures at the expense of the development of the soul, we are paying rent instead of making mortgage payments. At the end of the day, we will have nothing to show. When we prefer temporal pleasures at the expense of eternal ones, our soul cries out in anguish and frustration, "I could be yours forever. How can you turn your back on me for something so fleeting and shallow?"

Learning to enjoy the pleasures of the soul is a process of identifying with one's essential self. That is the work of a lifetime. A small child appreciates the taste of chocolate; only with the passage of years can he begin to appreciate more spiritual pleasures. As that "soul perspective" takes root, our physical existence becomes increasingly an expression of the needs of the soul and the means by which the soul is developed.

Our Sages compare this world to a vestibule — a waiting room — and the World to Come to a palace. "Prepare yourself in the vestibule," they say, "so that you will be able to enter the palace" (*Ethics of the Fathers* 4:21). With this metaphor, they do not devalue this world. It is the only path by which to reach the palace. Without the preparation in the vestibule, there is no entry into the palace.

Only insofar as we have developed our soul in this world can we enter the palace. But without the natural inclination for the pleasures of the body, there would be no struggle and no means for the soul to develop — in short, no way to enter the palace.

Now a person might argue that he is content with the pleasures of this world and has no interest in foregoing or curtailing them in order to enter the palace. He might even acknowledge that the pleasures of the palace are greater, but that he prefers his present pleasures, such as they are. Such an attitude is relatively commonplace today, as instant gratification takes precedence over sacrifice for some long-range goal.

In general there is not much one can say to a person who opts for instant gratification over delayed pleasure. But we must remember that we are not simply comparing two lollipops, one bigger and one smaller. A person who chooses the pleasures of the body over those of the soul is not just opting for a smaller bag of goodies; he is, in effect, destroying his essential self by preventing the soul from developing its potential.

Thus King Solomon compares the fool, one who eschews the development of the soul in favor of the pursuit of physical pleasures, to a man eating his own flesh (*Ecclesiastes* 4:5). His own flesh may be tasty, but as he consumes it, he consumes himself in the process.

When we recognize that our purpose in life is the development of our soul so that it can be a recipient of G-d's bounty, our whole approach to the events of this world changes radically. Now our question with respect to everything that life throws at us is no longer: "Would I have chosen this for myself?" Rather it is: "How can what is happening bring me closer to actualizing the potential of my soul, and thus bring me closer to the palace?"

Even suffering that appears undeserved in the context of reward and punishment can make sense in this framework. As long as it brings a person to develop his essential self, it fits into G-d's tapestry of purpose.

4 Suffering as Punishment

NOW THAT WE HAVE LAID THE NECESSARY FOUNDATIONS for our discussion, we can turn to the specific reasons for suffering delineated in our classical sources. We begin with suffering as punishment. By punishment we mean negative consequences — or at least consequences perceived by us as negative — that flow as a direct result of our own negative actions.

We start with punishment not because it is necessarily the most common reason for suffering, but because it is the explanation most readily assumed by a religious person, who believes in G-d's justice.

There is another reason to begin with punishment: It is so prone to being misunderstood. When we interpret our suffering as punishment, we feel rejected by G-d and unloved. That feeling of rejection and abandonment can be more devastating than whatever negative consequences we are currently experiencing. It is one thing to feel the sharpness of pain; it is another to experience the loneliness of being abandoned by G-d Himself.

IN THE PRECEDING CHAPTERS, WE ESTABLISHED THAT G-D created the world with a purpose. Our Sages tell us

Earned and Unearned Bread

that His purpose was none other than to shower us with good. Indeed they go further. Not only does He desire only to give to us, but, as the true giver, His focus is exclusively on the recipients of His beneficence. In other words, He wants to give to us in the way that is best for us.

When we first hear this formulation, however, it strikes us as hopelessly incomplete, even at odds with our own experience of the world. If everything exists only for our benefit, why is there so much pain and suffering? If G-d wants only our good, why does He allow us to experience so much bad?

To answer that question we must first understand what we mean when we say that G-d wants to give to us in the manner that will be best for us. Again our Sages supply the answer: Best for us means that we are somehow capable of earning G-d's gifts. What we receive without any effort or merit on our part, our

Sages describe as the "bread of embarrassment." According to the Talmud (*Yerushalmi Orlah* 1:3), when someone receives a gift that he has not earned, he is incapable of looking his benefactor in the face.[1]

A constant stream of unearned gifts exacts a very high cost from the recipient. Ultimately it drains him of his dignity and sense of self-worth. We all recognize this intuitively. As an occasional experience, we love being presented with a giant platter of cookies as soon as we enter Grandma's house. Those cookies have nothing to do with anything that we have done, and everything to do with Grandma's unconditional love. We enjoy the experience because it is occasional. But if it were constant, we would soon find it stifling. We would experience a lack of autonomy, an inability to develop a sense of self. Grandma's love would smother us.

Because He seeks our greatest good, G-d provides us with an opportunity to earn our greatest reward, which, as we have said, is a relationship with Him. As a nation, we experienced that relationship most intensely at Mount Sinai, when the Heavens opened up for a fleeting moment, and we became aware of G-d with all of our senses. There we "saw" the words of G-d, i.e., we experienced them with all the immediacy of sight.

How do we as individuals earn a relationship with G-d? By exercising our free will in a positive fashion.

---

1. The Hebrew term for face, *panim*, is related to *p'nim*, one's inner self. This lexical connection reflects a physiological truth: A person's inner depth shines through his face. If one cannot look his benefactor in the face, it means that he feels the need to hide something about himself and feels unworthy of the gift that he has just received. When a person has earned what he receives he does not experience any such embarrassment.

Each exercise of our free will, each choice that we make, shapes our inner self. It changes us for better or worse; it makes us a more spiritual person, and thus more capable of entering into a relationship with G-d, or a more physically bound person, with less capacity for such a relationship.

The ability to shape ourselves through our own free will is the necessary condition for a true relationship with G-d. In any relationship, we want to be loved by our partner for that which is most essential to ourselves. No deep relationship can be sustained, for instance, if we suspect that our partner is more interested in our money than in us. A woman does not wish to be loved solely for her physical appearance. She views her looks as external to her real self, and it is for the latter that she wishes to be loved.

If we could not choose, if all our decisions were automatic or compelled, we could not shape our inner selves. Indeed we would lack any individuality at all. Without any characteristics that were intrinsic to ourselves, and not imposed upon us from without, we could not be party to any relationship. Lacking a self, we could not be loved for that self.

Thus our free will is the necessary condition for us to receive G-d's greatest gift — a relationship with Him — in a manner that is not degrading and does not deprive us of our dignity. It is the precondition for any real relationship.

Rabbi Yitzchak Hutner emphasizes the importance of choice to our ability to earn Hashem's beneficence in his discussion of Psalm 136, which we read every

Shabbos morning in the *p'sukei d'zimra* section of the prayers. King David praises G-d for 26 acts of kindness that preceded the giving of the Torah at Sinai. Each verse concludes, "*ki l'olam chasdo,* for His kindness is eternal." These 26 verses correspond to the 26 generations from Adam to the giving of the Torah.

One might think, writes Rabbi Hutner, that G-d's kindness was greater during those 26 generations because it was totally unearned, like Grandma's cookies. But that would be a serious mistake. G-d's greatest kindness was the gift of the Torah, which made it possible to earn His beneficence by choosing to comply with His will as revealed in the Torah.

For choice to be meaningful, it must have consequences. Reward in the form of a relationship with G-d is the result of choosing to make ourselves worthy of that relationship. But like all choices, it has a flip side. That flip side is the negative consequences that we experience when we choose to alienate ourselves from G-d.

As WE HAVE SEEN, THE ABILITY TO SHAPE OURSELVES through our choices, and thus merit a relationship

Punishment and G-d's Kindness

with G-d, allows us to earn G-d's reward. For those choices to be real, they must involve consequences. Without consequences, we are deprived of our human dignity.

Viewed in this way, even punishment is an expression of G-d's love for us. It is a crucial aspect of a system designed so that we can receive G-d's good in the way that is best for us, without the shame of eating unearned bread.

Certainly G-d Himself gains nothing from those negative consequences. Just the opposite. On an individual level, every time a righteous person suffers, doubts are raised about G-d's justice and control of the world. And on a national level, when *Klal Yisrael* is forced into exile because of our sins, G-d's name is profaned. The defeat of His chosen people and their expulsion is perceived as a reflection, *chas v'shalom,* of G-d's own weakness. G-d, as it were, shoulders the insult in order to preserve the system of reward and punishment He established for our benefit.

Thus punishment too originates in G-d's giving and love for us. A *Midrash* (*Mechilta, Bereishis Shirah* 5) about Sodom makes this point clearly. The Torah describes G-d literally as raining, *himtir,* fire and brimstone on Sodom, and the *Midrash* is puzzled by the use of the verb for *causing to rain* with respect to brimstone. To resolve this difficulty, the *Midrash* concludes that G-d caused rain to fall from the Heavens but that it turned to brimstone below because that is what Sodom deserved.

The point of the *Midrash* is that whatever comes from G-d nourishes and sustains us like rain. Even when it is experienced by the recipient negatively — like brimstone — it still is for his benefit. G-d gives only good, but like any true giver, the manner in which His gifts reach the recipient are shaped by the specific needs of the recipient.

We acknowledge this reality when we recite the blessing "*Baruch dayan ha'emes,* Blessed is the true Judge," on bad news, just as we recite the blessing "*hatov ve'hameitiv,* Who is good and does good" upon hearing good news. When we say "*Baruch dayan ha'emes,*" we are telling G-d, "You are the perfect Judge. If this has happened, it must be that You judged it necessary for my needs, and I accept that judgment." At the same time, we cannot say, "*hatov ve'hameitiv.*" That would be insincere, for we lack the vantage point to see the good in whatever befalls us.

The perceived negative consequences that we call punishment have nothing to do with retribution, which is backward-looking. Rather they look to the future. Rabbi Moshe Chaim Luzzato and Rabbi Moshe Cordevero, two of our greatest mystical thinkers, both write that if punishment will not enable a person to receive greater good from G-d at some later point, He does not inflict it. Purely retributive punishment has no place in the Divine plan, which is to give man as much good as possible.

G-d does not punish us out of a desire to push us away, but rather out of a desire to make it possible for us to draw closer. The root of that punishment is love. In Yiddish when things are difficult, we say, "*G-tt handelt mit mir,* G-d is dealing with me." In this simple phrase, we recognize punishment as a proof of our ongoing relationship.

Understood in this way, we are in a much better position to accept the "bad" things that happen to us. Far from being a sign of G-d's abandonment, they reflect His desire to give to us. Our first emotional reaction is to curl up and feel rejected. But as hard as it is to move beyond such gut emotional responses, we must do so if we are to gain from the punishment.[2]

Still, we may wonder, if G-d's punishment flows directly from His love, why are there so many verses in the Torah and the Prophets where punishment of individuals or of the entire nation is portrayed as an outgrowth of G-d venting His wrath? What does His anger have to do with love?

We can best understand how the two are reconciled with an analogy. Imagine a father whose greatest desire in life is to give to his son. He wants to provide

---

2. There is an interesting hint in the halachah to the proper connection between punishment and love. When the Temple stood and Jewish courts still meted out the punishment of lashes, there were two requirements for those administering the lashes: they had to be weak and they had to be wise. The first requirement is easily understood as a reflection of the Torah's mercy. But why did the flogger need to be wise?

The requirement of wisdom derives from the importance of maintaining a proper perspective on the one receiving the lashes. The natural reaction is to define him entirely in terms of the transgression for which he receives lashes. The wise man, however, will view him in a more holistic fashion, i.e., as someone who may have done something wrong, but who nevertheless possesses many fine traits.

Apparently that difference in attitude is conveyed in the lashes themselves — a certain energy flows from the whip to the recipient's back. He can discern the difference between lashes of love and correction, and those of destruction and rejection.

The flogger as an agent of the court is also G-d's agent. As such, he must administer the lashes just as G-d metes out punishment: with a view of the totality of the person. G-d never loses sight of our great potential. Indeed it is only because of that great potential that He punishes at all. The punishment is designed to help the victim realize his fullest potential for a relationship with G-d.

(There is another crucial lesson to be derived from this halachah for parents. The effectiveness of parents' punishment depends primarily on the attitude that accompanies it. If they communicate to their child that he is "bad," he will likely fulfill their expectations. The punishment will only serve to drive him farther away. But if they communicate their appreciation of all his good qualities, even as they have identified something in his character or behavior that is obscuring some of them, he will be able to accept the punishment and incorporate its lessons.)

his son with money to go to yeshiva, to prepare himself for the most rewarding life possible — a life of Torah and *mitzvos*.

Unfortunately, the son is a drug addict. If his father were to give him money to go to yeshiva, it would be spent immediately on his habit. The money, rather than being an investment in the son's future, would only further his self-destruction.

The father has a clear vision of what would be best for his son, and he desperately wants to provide him with the means of fulfilling that vision. But he cannot do so because of the son's own failings. Imagine the father's frustration.

Hashem feels that same frustration, explains Rabbi Chaim Volozhin, when He is prevented from showering upon us every manner of blessing by our own inability to use those blessings properly. It is that frustration that the Torah refers to as G-d's anger.

The father in our story does not turn his back on his son. Instead he sends him to a grueling drug rehabilitation program. He would rather spend the money on his son for more positive things, but that is what his son needs at the moment.

Similarly, G-d does not turn His back upon us. He finds other means, some painful, to bring us to the point where we can receive what He so desperately wants to give us. When He is forced to do so, He feels, as it were, intense frustration. Not because He is our foe, but precisely because of His profound love for us and His desire to give us the greatest possible good.

SO FAR WE HAVE EXPLAINED HOW THE NEGATIVE CONSEQUENCES that follow from our own bad choices are necessary to

How Punishment Works

preserve the possibility of meaningful choice and with it our ability to earn reward from G-d. But it still remains to be seen how those negative consequences themselves benefit us, and actually facilitate our drawing closer to G-d.

To do that we will first have to correct a common misconception about the spiritual universe. We are used to thinking of the physical universe as operating according to fixed rules. Certain chemicals, for instance, mixed together under the proper conditions will inevitably explode. And certain poisons when drunk will inevitably lead to death or very serious illness.

But when we think about the spiritual universe, if we do so at all, we tend not to think in terms of such causal links between our deeds and the spiritual consequences they entail. When we do something forbidden by the Torah, we acknowledge that we have transgressed G-d's Will, but we do not assume that any consequences follow automatically from that transgression in the same way that they follow from swallowing poison. Rather we attribute any adverse consequences that flow from our transgression to G-d's independent decision to be strict with us.

That is a fundamental misunderstanding of the nature of the spiritual world. That world operates according to its own set of detailed rules, in which certain actions entail certain spiritual consequences, as surely as swallowing poison results in extreme nausea.

If we pursue the analogy to swallowing poison a bit further, we might picture sin as introducing spiritual toxins into our system. The Hebrew word for spiritual impurity, *tumah,* is from a root that refers to being blocked or stopped up. That is what our transgressions do; they block our souls from their source in G-d.

Adam HaRishon is the paradigm for this model of sin creating spiritual blockages. Prior to eating of the fruit Adam was immortal. Eating of the fruit of the Tree of Knowledge introduced mortality into the world. Why was that? What was the connection between violating G-d's explicit commandment and death?

Rabbi Moshe Chaim Luzzato explains the connection. Prior to eating of the fruit, Adam's soul and body coexisted without tension, and the body's subservience to the soul was clear. Therefore just as the soul was immortal so was the body.

When he ate of the fruit, Adam for the first time experienced his body as something distinct from his soul. For the first time, writes Reb Tzadok HaKohen (*Kuntres Eis HaOchel*), he experienced physical pleasure as an end in itself, unconnected to any spiritual purpose. In the process, the body grew independent of the soul, and subject to the processes of the physical world — decay and death. Death, then, was the consequence of man now being cut off from his spiritual root.

The consequences of introducing toxins into our spiritual universe parallel what happens when we swallow something that is bad for us. We experience acute nausea. That nausea is the immediate consequence of eating something that is bad for us or of eating too much. It might be called the punishment for overeating. But the vomiting that follows, as unpleasant as it may be, serves a valuable purpose: it allows us to eject the poison from our body.

In the spiritual realm as well, we experience direct consequences from the introduction of spiritual poisons into our system. Those consequences are designed to remove the threat to our spiritual existence, i.e., the blockage between soul and body. Removal of that blockage inevitably entails pain, as does the excision of anything that has become part of us.

The reaction of our spiritual immune system is not unlike the nausea that follows imbibing poison. It is our own reaction to the blockage we have created between our bodies and souls by having placed too great a stress on our physical side. That stress on the physical deadens us spiritually, and reduces our capacity to maintain a relationship with G-d.[3] Fortunately, G-d has created us with corrective mechanisms to right the imbalance. Those mechanisms are the spiritual equivalent of the nausea caused by poison.

When the negative consequences that flow from our transgressions are viewed in this way, we can readily grasp the answer to a nagging question: Granted we may not have done everything that G-d

---

3. Once we identify the primary source of the blockage between ourselves and our spiritual selves as the overemphasis on the physical aspect of our being, it becomes clear that suffering is not the only possible corrective.

Suffering helps wean us of our infatuation with the physical side of our existence, but there are other ways to achieve the same results. If a person recognizes himself that he has damaged himself, he can take corrective action by emphasizing the spiritual side of his being and eschewing the

wanted from us, but what would be so terrible if He chose to overlook our transgressions? If He so greatly desires our good, why not be lenient? It wouldn't cost Him anything.

We have already given one answer to this question at the philosophical level. G-d cannot overlook the consequences of our wrong choices without undermining the significance of correct choices. Choices without consequences are not real choices. To remove the consequences then would be to deprive us of the dignity for which we were given free will in the first place.

But now we can see that there is a far more direct, practical answer to the question. Overlooking our transgressions would leave the spiritual blockages intact. Those blockages are the natural consequence of our choice to disobey G-d, and will plague us so long as the blockage is not removed.

Once that blockage has been created, sparing us the unpleasantness of removing it would be an act of cruelty, not of mercy. Overlooking that spiritual blockage would be comparable to a doctor refusing to pump the stomach of someone who had swallowed poison in order to spare him discomfort. Such a doctor would be guilty of gross malpractice.

The only reason that we fail to see this is that we remain stuck in a framework in which the physical

---

selfish pursuit of pleasure. He might, for instance, begin learning more, giving more charity, doing more to help others, give up luxuries, sleep less.

While such a course requires a deep commitment, it might well substitute for the pain of suffering. Since, in any event, the punishment we are describing is forward-looking, not retributive, our own actions that achieve the same results as suffering can serve as substitutes.

world operates according to fixed rules while the spiritual world operates without any parallel calculus of cause and effect. We acknowledge that there are consequences of our actions, but view those consequences as imposed by G-d on a case by case basis, and not according to any spiritual "rules of nature."

But when we understand that there are spiritual rules, and that certain actions inevitably entail particular consequences, we can also understand why G-d cannot just overlook our transgressions: We have poisoned ourselves, and we must be cured. The purgative may be painful, but there is no other way forward. That is what our Sages mean when they say, "Whoever says that *HaKodosh Baruch Hu* overlooks [sin], may his bowels be relaxed" (i.e., may he die) (*Yalkut Shimoni Bereishis* 115).

The Hebrew word for punishment, *onesh*, conveys this sense of punishment as the removal of a blockage. It derives from the same root as *nashoh*, which means to move from its place. *Onesh,* then, is designed to remove the blockage that follows from transgression. As we have noted before, it looks forward, towards reestablishing the connection between soul and body, between ourselves and G-d.

The punishment we are discussing thus has nothing in common with the Western concept of punishment as retribution and/or deterrence: "Now you are really going to get it in a way that expresses our outrage at what you have done and will make you or others think twice before doing the same thing again."

But if punishment is forward-looking, as we have argued, how can we account for suffering that terminates in death? What good has the suffering done where there is no more future in which to incorporate the lessons of that suffering and to reestablish the relationship with G-d?

At least intellectually, if not emotionally, the answer to that question should be clear from what we have said earlier (see Chapter 3). The "future" about which we are speaking is not exclusively, nor even primarily, in this world; nor is the ultimate relationship with G-d in this world. Rather it is the eternal relationship in the World to Come, which is the outgrowth of what we have achieved in this world. That reward is received by the essential aspect of ourselves, the soul, after the outer shell of the body has been shed. Thus our suffering can be the prelude to a closer relationship with G-d, even where it ends in death.

King David makes this point. He lived a life filled with travail: he spent years fleeing from King Shaul; he buried children; his own sons rebelled against him and tried to kill him. Yet he proclaimed, "G-d's wrath is but a moment, life is His true desire" (*Psalms* 30:6).

So much of his life was spent in sorrow, and yet he described G-d's wrath as but a fleeting moment. How can that be? Because, say the commentators, he viewed his entire seventy years in this world as but a fleeting moment compared to the eternity of the soul. And he recognized true life as the life of the soul, for which the events of this world were only a preparation. G-d's true desire is "life" — the life of the soul enjoying a closeness to Him for eternity.

OUR OWN CHOICES SEPARATE US FROM G-D. PUNISHMENT IS the cure for that separation, the means by which the

Adam HaRishon as Paradigm of Separation and Reconciliation

barriers are removed. *Adam HaRishon* is the paradigm for this process of distancing and reconciliation.

In the Garden of Eden, Adam felt himself in intimate proximity to G-d. He was aware of G-d with a degree of clarity unimaginable to us. For Adam, his relationship with G-d was a given. His task was only to preserve that relationship, not to create it.

Yet Adam deliberately destroyed that relationship by violating the only commandment that he had been given. He reasoned that he could better serve G-d when G-d's presence was obscured (see Chapter 1).

To what can we compare this? Imagine two newlyweds in the blissful days immediately after their marriage, still completely enthralled with one another. Then suddenly the husband says to his wife, "I think we are getting too close." She is devastated. He has introduced distance into their relationship for the first time.

Seeing her shock, he may be filled with remorse, but the words are out of his mouth, and they cannot be returned. There is no possibility of pretending that they were not said. The husband requires more than just forgiveness to heal the wound. He has introduced distance into the relationship, and if he wishes to reestablish the past closeness, he must repair it himself. The breach must be recognized and corrected. Only by demonstrating how much he wants the relationship can the husband hope to attain the former closeness. That closeness can no longer be assumed; it must be created again.

Similarly, Adam had to repair his turning away from G-d. That turning away became incorporated into his soul, and its repair required a similar turning towards G-d. That could not take place in Gan Eden. There G-d was too close. There the relationship existed automatically.

If he was to heal the wound, Adam had to seek out a relationship. But he could only do that if he was first expelled from the Garden of Eden. Only the punishment of expulsion made it possible for Adam to actively seek out a relationship.

All transgression places a barrier between us and G-d; it is the equivalent of our saying to G-d, "We are getting too close." The distance placed between ourselves and G-d now requires us to seek Him. He pushes us away not because He wants that distance, but in order to force us to actively pursue the relationship with Him that is sundered by our transgression.

ROSH HASHANAH IS A PUZZLING DAY FOR US. ON THE ONE hand, we are facing an awesome judgment; on the

Approaching Rosh Hashanah

other hand, we celebrate the day as a joyous holiday. One can hardly imagine someone facing a life and death judgment enjoying himself the preceding night. Yet that is what we do.

More than that. We not only celebrate amidst the judgment, we actually invoke the judgment on ourselves. The shofar summons the Judge to the chamber to begin the proceedings. Clearly we would only do so if we viewed that judgment as beneficial to us.

A *Midrash* concerning Rosh Hashanah makes this point. Rosh Hashana falls on the first of *Tishrei,* says the *Midrash*, because it was then that *Adam HaRishon* was judged favorably. That first favorable judgment serves as a hopeful precedent for our own judgment.

How was Adam judged favorably? we might ask. As a consequence of his sin, he lost his immortality and death was introduced into the world. Chava was condemned to suffer the pains of childbirth, and Adam to earn his bread by the sweat of his brow.

The answer, the *Midrash* suggests, is that the very act of judgment itself was favorable because it showed that G-d still cared about the relationship. G-d visited upon Adam the consequences of his actions in order to preserve the overall system of consequences.

Recognizing that G-d's judgment itself is a sign of our ongoing relationship does not, however, remove our apprehension about that judgment. To ignore those feelings would be insincere. Even as we rejoice in the larger context within which the judgment is taking place, we do not lose sight of what is at stake.

That ambiguity is hinted to in Nechemiah's instructions to the exiles returning from Babylonia the first Rosh Hashanah after their return. They began to weep when they realized that their sins had led to the exile. In response, Nechemiah told them, "Eat fat meat and drink sweet wine ... for *joy* in G-d is your strength." The Holy Tongue has many terms for joy. That employed by Nechemiah was *chedvah*.

We find a verb of the same root in the Torah to describe Yisro's rejoicing upon hearing of the miracles that accompanied the Children of Israel as they left Egypt, including the drowning of the Egyptians at the Sea: "And Yisro rejoiced" (*Exodus* 18:9). Yisro was originally from Egypt, where he served as an advisor to Pharoah. Later, Yisro joined the Jewish people, and bound his fate to theirs. At the deepest level, he rejoiced at the destruction of Egypt, for that destruction was the means by which G-d revealed Himself to the entire world. Yet he also felt sadness for his former people drowned at the Sea.

Chedvah conveys that sense of a deeper joy, with an admixture of sadness. And it is that mixture that we feel on Rosh Hashanah. Indeed whenever "G-d is 'dealing' with us" we face the same mixture of sadness and joy. At the most immediate level, we are acutely aware of our pain. But at the deepest level, we experience satisfaction in the knowledge of G-d's ongoing concern for us and of His desire to give that underlies our current suffering.

We must emphasize again that not all, or even most, suffering is punishment. It is only one of the many reasons for suffering found in our sources. Nevertheless we must come to grips with the possibility of punishment. That requires recognizing the reality of our relationship with G-d, and the consequences that flow from our actions. Only when we accept those consequences of our actions are we capable of growing. When we distance ourselves from G-d, we have to draw close once again. When the lines of communication have become blocked, they must be cleared to allow for the free flow of relationship once again.

5 DIVINE JUSTICE

WE HAVE EXPLAINED THE THEORETICAL FRAMEWORK within which we can understand how a giving G-d utilizes punishment as a constructive element in His overall relationship to Creation. When faced with the details of suffering, however, we still have many questions which make it difficult for us to accept that G-d's justice is perfect and that He directs the world only for our good.

FACED WITH SUFFERING, WE QUESTION THE WHOLE LOGIC OF punishment. Granted that a price must be paid for

An Unreasonable Exchange

transgressions. But if everything is for our benefit, isn't there a better way for G-d to deal with us? After all, we are basically decent people. We may have done some things wrong, but we can think of a lot more good that we have done. Why can't G-d just subtract the bad from the good and leave us with a net surplus of good?

We would like to tell G-d, "I know I'm not perfect, but I am a nice person. There were things that I could have done better; there were a few things that were definitely wrong. But if You tally all the results, on the whole I am good. Maybe I can think of three real mistakes, but I can come up with at least ten good deeds. Subtract the three from the ten and give me a reward for the seven. Why must I suffer?"

If we keep in mind the function of punishment, we can answer this question. We explained that transgression changes us in a way that prevents us from developing a complete relationship with G-d: We introduce something negative into our system which blocks our connection with the Higher Realm. Punishment repairs the damage by cleansing us, or altering our circumstances, to allow for the continued development of our relationship with G-d.

If transgressions only caused the equivalent of a pain in the toe — if they merely restricted incidental activities, while leaving us functioning normally — then we could talk about trading a transgression for a good deed. But transgression cripples the whole system.

By tying us more closely to the physical world, it hampers us in our attempt to draw close to G-d. Trying to reach G-d while still under the influence of our misdeeds is like trying to understand a profound discussion under the influence of a powerful sedative.

The effects of transgression must be erased in order for us to experience the rewards for our good deeds. We must shake off the sedative, so to speak. That is what punishment does; it reduces our attachment to the physical aspects of life.

Good deeds and sins exist on two completely different planes. Thus one can no more be subtracted from the other than apples from oranges. Good deeds are expressions of the soul projected onto the physical world. They reflect our connection to an infinite level of being and bind us to G-d. Sin, on the other hand, is an expression of our over-attachment to the finite, physical world.

Because good deeds express our eternal essence, their reward is eternal. Because our transgressions are related to the physical and transitory within us, their consequences need not reach beyond the finite time frame of this world. To trade a good deed for a sin is like sticking a gold coin in a soda machine. If the coin is the right size, it will buy you a can of soda. But a soda only costs a quarter while the gold coin can buy a palace. In His kindness, G-d refuses to take the gold coins of our good deeds to pay off the debts incurred for our transgressions.

THE CONCEPT OF COMPARING OUR GOOD DEEDS TO OUR transgressions is found in the Talmud and Maimonides.

The Balance Sheet The accounting of which they speak, however, is not for the purpose of determining one's reward and punishment. Rather it is designed to establish a person's essence: Is this person basically good, his life characterized by the pursuit of G-d, with occasional moments of selfishness? Or does he live for himself, doing some good once in a while? That judgment is made by weighing his positive and negative deeds against one another.

That evaluation must of necessity precede the determination of reward and punishment. If one is essentially a seeker of G-d, his righteous deeds express his essence, while his selfish deeds are only tangentially related to that essence. His negative actions, however, reflect only a superficial aspect of his personality.

The determination of a person's essence affects his ultimate reward and punishment. Acts which express our essence are rewarded in the next world, where we exist without our bodies. In this world, our bodies hide our true selves. Not only do these bodies deceive others as to our true nature, they often deceive us as well. But in the World to Come all facades fall away and we stand revealed for who we truly are. There only the basic self continues to exist, and only the deeds which express that essential self are relevant. By contrast, this world is the appropriate place for an accounting for those deeds which express the nonessential side of ourselves.

One who was in essence a seeker of G-d in this world has formed himself into a being worthy of an eternal relationship with G-d. The reward of the next world is the experience of that relationship with G-d.

Such a person's transgressions are only loosely connected to him; they do not express his true self. He must, of course, pay for his misdeeds, but since they do not express his essence, he pays for them in the fleeting realm of this world. His punishment ends in this world. His reward is saved for the next.

On the other hand, one who lives his life with an eye only to what he can grab for himself, whose selfish acts express his true essence, reaps the results of his selfishness in the next world. He creates for himself an existence separate from G-d. Such an existence is nothingness. In the next world, he will experience the non-existence he has created. His few good deeds, on the other hand, which are incidental to his primary self, will be rewarded in the currency of this world.

A person's essence is evaluated on Rosh Hashanah. On that day, the Book of Life and the Book of Death are opened. Life and Death, in this case, do not refer to biological life and death, but rather to whether one is joined to the source of Eternal Life — to G-d Himself. The Book of Life includes all those who are truly alive in the sense of being joined to a larger infinite reality. The Book of Death, on the other hand, includes the walking dead — those who live in a world where G-d is absent. That is what our Sages mean when they say, "The righteous are called living, even in death, and the wicked are called dead even in life" (*Yerushalmi Berachos* 2:3).

After this evaluation of our essence on Rosh Hashanah, we are ready for Yom Kippur, the day on which the details of our reward and punishment are fixed. Rosh Hashanah determines the level at which our reward and punishment are meted out. That does not mean, however, that one is destined for a year of comfort just because he was inscribed in the Book of Life. Precisely because a person seeks an intense relationship with G-d, he might suffer in this world. That suffering burns away the dross clouding his relationship with G-d.

THE MOST DIFFICULT CHALLENGE TO OUR BELIEF IN PUNISHMENT as perfect divine justice is the age-old question[1]: Why

Why the Righteous Suffer

do we frequently witness the righteous suffering while the wicked prosper?

If no one were happy in this world, perhaps we could accept the suffering of the righteous. But that is not so. We all know plenty of people who reject or are indifferent to G-d who nevertheless appear to be leading perfectly happy lives. And we know others whose lives are devoted to G-d and yet endure horrible suffering. This is deeply troubling to the believer, for it undermines his ability to accept the justice of Divine punishment.

To deal with these feelings, we must first recognize that the primary reward for those who pursue a

---

1. Moshe also asked this question of G-d. See *Berachos* 7a.

relationship with G-d is in the World to Come. There his essential self receives an eternal reward. Yet even the most righteous person inevitably slips into instances of selfishness in this world. If not purged in this world, those actions constitute a barrier to the fullest relationship with G-d in the next world. Suffering purges those expressions of one's non-essential self in this world.

The wicked, on the other hand, are basically selfish. They will reap their punishment in the World to Come. Their good deeds reflect the more superficial aspect of their selves, and are therefore rewarded in this world, which is transitory and therefore less important.[2]

None of the foregoing should be taken to mean that all those who are comfortable in this world are wicked, while all those who suffer are righteous. Righteous, in the sense we are using it, covers a broad spectrum — all those who are destined for a good life in the next world. That includes many people who are incapable of growing from suffering. In addition, there are those who are so righteous that they are not punished at all, and those so wicked that they are punished in both this world and the next.

In short, there are many factors involved in each particular situation. Although we know the general principles, we are incapable for the most part of identifying precisely what is happening in any particular case. We will have to be satisfied with a theoretical framework that accounts for the pain of the

---

2. *Ramban, Shaar HaGemul*

righteous, and yet allows us to retain our belief in divine justice.

THERE IS ANOTHER WRINKLE TO BE CONSIDERED IN OUR evaluation of Divine justice:

Who is Righteous? We are not always capable of distinguishing someone who is really righteous from someone who merely appears to be righteous. Sometimes, we are overly generous in judging someone to be a *tzaddik*. Though we are required to judge others favorably, there is no requirement to be naive. Too much naivete may skew our vision of how divine justice operates.

We all know that a long white beard and a front seat in the synagogue are not necessarily perfect measures of righteousness. And even someone who is genuinely virtuous in all his public activities may present a sharply contrasting persona in private. Rabbis, for instance, get to know people on many levels. Many people are sweet, considerate, and charming to the rabbi; in fact, they are sweet, considerate, and charming to everyone right down to the long-distance operator and the toll collector. But when the rabbi talks to their wives, he hears a very different description.

Rabbi Chaim Vital, a great sixteenth-century Kabbalist, writes that G-d judges men by how they treat their wives much more than by how they treat others. A man can present a mask to the outside world. No matter how perfect the mask, it still does not represent his true self. But he cannot hide behind a mask with his wife. She is a part of himself and it is only to her that he reveals his true self. If he is cruel to her, that cruelty more accurately reflects his true self. He controls it publicly because he is concerned about his image. But his wife sees his real self, and it is that self which G-d evaluates.

It is helpful to remember that G-d's definition of righteousness is not the same as ours. We are likely to give high marks to anyone who is generally pleasant, pays his debts on time, doesn't get on our nerves, and adds a bit of cheer to our lives. G-d, however, did not create us merely to pass time pleasantly. He seeks to give us all that He can give. That, in turn, requires us to develop all the resources with which He imbued us. G-d measures us against our potential and He will not compromise on our fully developing that potential. We cannot know anyone else's potential, and therefore have no way of determining the standard by which he is being judged.

OUR ABILITY TO PERCEIVE G-D'S JUSTICE IS COMPLICATED BY the fact that each person is judged by his own personal yardstick. Two people can commit the same act and yet elicit two very different responses from G-d. That is because each person is born with different capabilities, and each person is judged according to those capabilities.

Identical Acts are Not Always the Same

If the righteous had their occasional slips overlooked, we could perhaps understand. Even in human courts, the judge often considers a man's overall character in determining punishment. Yet that is not how G-d metes out punishment. We are taught that the opposite is true: G-d is exacting with the righteous to a hairsbreadth (*Yevamos* 121b).

To understand why, we must remember that G-d seeks to push each person to the realization of his full potential. We are judged in light of the capabilities with which we were endowed. Those with greater potential are judged in a more exacting fashion because of their greater potential. Increased potential brings with it increased responsibility. G-d does not give a person certain abilities in order to make his life easier. Talents are meant to be employed for the good of the community.

Throughout history, the great men of Israel achieved what they did not solely because of their extraordinary gifts, but because of their sense of responsibility to develop their gifts and use them on behalf of others. David was king of all Israel. He could have lounged in bed well into the morning, as was the custom of royalty in his day. Instead he would arise at midnight and sing praises to G-d until morning (*Berachos* 4a). Even today the greatest Torah scholars wipe sleep from their eyes and push themselves to learn until very late at night. One great rabbi almost lost his job in Eastern Europe because some members of the community walked past his home at night and did not see a candle burning. They did not realize that he was too poor to even afford candles. That was the attitude in Europe. Any *rav* who does not learn until the wee hours of the morning is no *rav*.

There is another aspect to the exacting standards by which the righteous man is judged. Our essence is our soul. Yet most of us remain unconscious of that fact most of the time. Our concerns center around our physical existence. The *tzaddik,* however, is more spiritually developed and operates on a different plane. He never forgets that his soul is his essence and he directs his energies accordingly.

His soul-consciousness gives his every action more far-reaching ramifications. The prayers of the righteous have a greater effect than those of someone who is less righteous. And conversely, the transgressions of the righteous cause greater damage than those misdeeds of the less righteous. Since punishment is designed to correct the imbalance caused by our sins, the *tzaddik,* or righteous man, is punished more harshly, for his sins cause greater imbalance.

The unusual power of a *tzaddik* explains another anomaly of divine justice. Sometimes we suffer as the result of others' sins. The classic example is Adam. Adam was created immortal. With his sin, however, he brought death not only upon himself, but upon all his descendants. Mankind is subject to death because of Adam. How is that just? We didn't do anything.

Adam's soul encompassed all of humanity. Every one who would ever be born possesses a piece of Adam's soul. When he distanced himself from G-d, inevitably, he took all of mankind along with him, for each individual's soul is a piece of Adam's soul. When Adam severed a particular connection to G-d, he severed the tie for everyone. Just as Adam had to die to repair the tear between him and G-d, so do we.

We might protest that this is unfair. We did not do anything wrong; we were born this way. Why must we suffer? But remember, punishment is always purposeful. If death is required to achieve a full relationship with G-d, then death there will be. If someone lives in a polluted area, his lungs will be blackened. When his doctor tells him that he must act to clean his lungs, it will do no good to protest that he did not pollute the air. Black lungs are black lungs, and they need to be dealt with. Similarly, we have inherited a spiritually tainted world. That is our reality, and we must work within the confines of that reality.

Once we recognize that great individuals can affect the entirety of existence, we can begin to understand another disturbing element in our perception of divine justice. The Torah mentions a number of seemingly small transgressions that resulted in extremely severe punishments. When G-d promised Avraham that he would be given the Land of Israel, Avraham asked, "How will I know that I will inherit it?" (*Genesis* 15:8). Clearly Avraham was not asking G-d to prove His promise. Nor did he doubt G-d's promise for a moment. (On these points all the commentators agree.) Rather, Avraham was concerned that he or his descendants might prove unworthy of the promise. And he wanted some sign that the promise would nevertheless be fulfilled. Possibly Avraham sought assurance that his descendants would remain sufficiently faithful to G-d to retain their claim to the Land. In short, Avraham wasn't questioning G-d; he was questioning himself.

Yet the commentaries detect in Avraham's question some minute lack of perfect faith in G-d. If G-d chose Avraham and his progeny to be His people, then Avraham should have known that G-d would not allow them to decline to a point where they would be incapable of fulfilling that mission.

Obviously, we are dealing with a very subtle failure on Avraham's part. Yet the Talmud (*Nedarim* 32a) makes the shocking claim that the entire Egyptian exile was designed solely to correct the absence of faith implied in Avraham's question. One minor failure — a failure too fine for us to even detect — brought hundreds of years of bitter suffering and exile upon an entire nation.

But Avraham was not just the man Avraham. He was not a world unto himself. He was the foundation upon which the entire Jewish people was built. Any fault in the foundation, however slight, manifests itself throughout the building. Foundations must be perfect. If left uncorrected, a fault in the foundation will undermine the entire structure.

The subtle separation from G-d revealed by Avraham's request for a tangible sign needed to be rectified completely, and that required more than two centuries of exile and slavery in Egypt.

UNTIL NOW, WE HAVE SPOKEN ABOUT SUFFERING AS A corrective and cleansing process. There is, however,

A Wake-up Call another aspect of suffering within the general category of punishment: Pain designed to wake us up. That pain alerts us that things are not right with our lives and that we must do something about it. At times, such wake-up calls are sudden and dramatic. Often they are out of the ordinary. They need not last for long because their purpose is to jolt us out of our spiritual slumber — to force us to stop and take stock of our lives.

Cleansing suffering must be carefully tailored to the particular spiritual toxins that we have imbibed. It is as personalized as a doctor's prescription in terms of dosage and length of therapy. A wake-up call, however, depends upon our response to the alarm. Its power and duration depend upon what it takes to shock us into awareness. Ignoring these calls is the spiritual equivalent of pushing the snooze button on an alarm clock. Like pushing the snooze button, ignoring the wake-up call is but a temporary solution: The alarm will sound again in a short while.

Punishment which comes to cleanse is administered with love. We do not receive an overdose. Every bit of the suffering removes blockages and the pain is carefully matched to the needs and strength of the recipient. A wake-up call, on the other hand, is meant to startle. It must be overwhelming. When you wake someone from a deep sleep, you cannot pat him tenderly on the head or whisper a lullaby in his ear. You need to shock him with loud noises or a splash of cold water. The sleeper does not like being wrenched out of a pleasant slumber, but there is no choice. Try a gentler approach, and he will open his eyes, give you a bleary-eyed look, and go back to sleep.

Modern man has many sophisticated ways to turn off G-d's wake-up calls and return to his spiritual slumber. Statistics are one such refuge: Such and such a percentage of people are stricken with this disease or are involved in these kinds of accidents, so there is no need to view them as a tailor-made wake up call. In this way, the subject of the wake-up call convinces himself that it has nothing to do with him — he just happens to fall in the unlucky percentage. Statistics thus tend to obscure Divine Providence.

Maimonides says a perplexing thing about people who deny Divine Providence. They have chosen a path of cruelty, writes Maimonides. Not intellectually misguided or lacking in faith, but cruel. Because the longer we ignore G-d's wake-up calls, the stronger they become. The sole purpose of such suffering is to awaken us, and the sooner we do so the sooner it will be over. Our own stubbornness thus causes us extra pain for no appreciable gain. That is cruelty to ourselves.

Wake-up calls force us to recognize that we are destroying ourselves. Once we have done so, we are in a position to regret the past and commit ourselves to a new course for the future — in short, to repent and do *teshuvah*. This is the preferred path — when we correct the imbalances within ourselves. By exercising our free will to change, we avoid much of the suffering required to remove the spiritual toxins.

Repentance allows us to open new channels of relationship with G-d instead of following the more arduous process of trying to unplug channels that have become obstructed. Like suffering that cleanses, that which serves as a wake-up call is motivated by love. By stimulating us to change and refashion our connection to G-d, it enables us to avoid the whole process of medicinal suffering.

6

Suffering as Character Building

NTIL NOW WE HAVE BEEN DISCUSSING SUFFERING AS punishment. When we are unable, as a consequence of our actions, to form a full relationship with G-d, He places us in difficult situations designed to help us repair ourselves and, in the process, recover our relationship to Him.

But, as we said at the outset, not all suffering is punishment. Our Sages also speak of *yisurim shel ahavah* — afflictions of love. As is the case with punishment, "afflictions of love" are also catalysts for personal growth, with one crucial difference: In the latter case the suffering is not designed to repair something that is blocked, but rather to uncover untapped potential.

Only through concrete actions do we form our character and realize our potential. Many of us fantasize, for instance, about being confronted with an overwhelming temptation and yet heroically resisting and remaining true to our principles. Such fantasies may, at least, reflect our good intentions, and for that there may be some reward. But we do not develop our character by fantasizing.

Only through choosing to act in a particular fashion is character formed. Human beings are complex bundles of conflicting desires. Often we find ourselves torn between those conflicting desires, and we are forced to choose between them. Those choices define who we are.

Suppose someone says to me, "Here is $100,000. All I ask is that you exaggerate slightly in court tomorrow," and I throw the money back at him. I have grown in the process; I have chosen between my desire for the money and my commitment to honesty. When the commitment to honesty prevails, the commitment itself is strengthened in the process. By acting repeatedly in such a fashion, I become an honest person. Only by exercising our power to choose do we grow.

Each of us brings hidden potential with him or her into the world. Often we ourselves are not aware of our untapped potential — our reserves of strength, hidden talents, and courage. Only when we are pressed up against the wall and forced to dig deep within ourselves do we discover strengths we never knew we possessed.

G-d sometimes makes our lives difficult to help us release that potential. Such suffering has nothing to do with punishment; it is not a response to anything we have done wrong. Rather we are being pushed to develop our potential. The *Midrash* (*Yalkut Shimoni Yirmiyahu* 289) compares the Jew to an olive. Just as the olive must be crushed in order to produce olive oil, so our potential is only fully realized under pressure.

Even though we recognize that suffering may offer us the potential for growth, however, most of us would probably choose not to reach our fullest potential rather than suffer. Here it is crucial that we return to our first principles and remember the purpose for which G-d created us: to shower upon us as much of His bounty as possible. That bounty — a relationship with Him — provides our lives with meaning. Without it, our lives become hollow and empty.

We must remember also that no matter how immediate and sharp our pain it is of limited duration. That suffering is a temporal investment toward an eternal reward. It would be the height of foolishness to reject a reward that is eternal. G-d does not give us the choice of passing up that everlasting reward by foregoing present pain.

Knowledge that all suffering does not result from punishment is crucial. Too often we interpret painful or tragic experiences as a message from G-d: "If G-d is doing this to me, I must be bad in His eyes." Such interpretations leave us feeling abandoned by G-d and foster a sense of inadequacy. On the other hand, if we conclude that we have done nothing to deserve such punishment, we may become angry with G-d for His perceived unfairness.

Recognition that these are "afflictions of love" helps us avoid both these reactions: the feeling of being rejected by G-d and the desire to reject G-d out of anger. When we appreciate that our pain may be part of a regimen to develop hidden potential, our sense of ourselves is lifted, not diminished. G-d is telling us that He believes in us, and that we possess many good qualities that need to be developed.

The greater the person, the more likely he is to suffer "afflictions of love." Avraham brought knowledge of G-d to the entire world and became the forefather of G-d's chosen people. Yet he suffered tests that would have broken anyone else. G-d visited these afflictions on Avraham not because he had sinned in any way, but to develop all the potential that would be handed down as a spiritual inheritance to Avraham's descendants.

Our Sages (*Midrash Tanchuma Vayeira* 20) compare the testing of a *tzaddik* to the beating of flax. Only the best flax can withstand a thorough beating. Such flax becomes softer and softer with each subsequent beating. Flax of lesser quality, however, could not be beaten in this fashion without being broken. That is not to say that only righteous people on the level of Avraham ever experience "afflictions of love." Wherever there exists potential, there exists the possibility of such suffering.

AFTER WE HAVE SURVIVED A TEST, IT IS NATURAL FOR US TO turn to G-d and thank Him. But if we sensitize our-

Thanking G-d for the Pain

selves to the ways in which our trials have caused us to grow, we will thank G-d not only for having helped us pass the test, but for the test itself. Whatever suffering was entailed by the test has caused us to become something more than we were previously.

The servitude of the Jewish people in Egypt illustrates the point. When Moses first petitioned Pharaoh for the release of the Jews, Pharaoh responded by immediately increasing their burden. Moses was dismayed to see his mission result in the direct opposite of what he hoped to achieve and complained directly to G-d: "*Meaz basi el Pharaoh … hera la'am hazeh,* From the moment I came to Pharaoh … things have only grown worse for this people …" (*Exodus* 5:23).

When the Jews crossed the Sea and saw the bodies of the Egyptians washed up on the shore, Moses led the people in singing G-d's praises. That song of praise begins with the word **Az**, meaning "at that moment." The same word that previously introduced Moses' complaint against G-d was now employed to sing G-d's praises. Even the suffering that engendered the earlier complaint was now seen as an additional cause for singing to G-d at the Sea. Moses sang in praise of G-d both for the suffering and the subsequent salvation.

We find a similar idea in *Psalms* when King David sings to G-d: "I will hold You in a high place, G-d, for You have humbled me" (*Psalms* 30:2). At first glance the verse is puzzling: Why should King David extol G-d for having humbled him?

The answer, explains *Ibn Ezra*, is that David intuitively understood the concept of "afflictions of love." He knew better than anyone that but for the never-ending succession of trials that he confronted he would never have become King David, progenitor of *Mashiach*.

Yet even King David's later recognition of the role played by his trials in his growth only provides limited solace at the moment of our suffering. King David was acknowledging the benefit of his trials looking back. But what are we to do while that suffering is still a present reality and not just a past memory? Should we laugh? Cry?

Here our forefather Avraham is the model. Avraham was tested ten times, say our Sages. The final test is known as the Binding of Isaac. Avraham was required to bind his beloved son Yitzchak, the only child of Sarah, on the Altar, presumably with the intent of slaying Yitzchak. G-d wanted to display to the world Avraham's willingness to sacrifice his son Yitzchak out of unquestioning devotion to G-d. Once Avraham had proved that willingness beyond all shadow of a doubt, an angel appeared and told him to stop immediately and to untie Yitzchak.

But how did Avraham feel the moment before the angel told him to stay his hand, as his arm was still uplifted over his son to slay him? The *Midrash* (*Bereishis Rabbah* 56:8) captures the scene. Avraham looked into Yitzchak's eyes and Yitzchak into his. At that moment, Avraham broke down and the tears poured down his cheeks. Nevertheless, says the *Midrash*, Avraham's heart rejoiced in his ability to act in accord with Hashem's will.

Avraham was human, and this situation demanding weeping. He was about to experience the most painful loss possible as a direct consequence of his own act of free will. Yet Avraham also knew that an aspect of greatness was being expressed through his choice. That elevated spiritual level could not emerge in any other circumstance — i.e., there could be no greater test. Even as the tears poured from his eyes, something deep inside him celebrated the sanctification of G-d that was taking place through him.

From Avraham we learn two things: We must be true to our feelings and admit our pain, for our suffering is real. Yet, at the same time, we must recognize that some aspect of ourselves previously hidden, and existing only in potential, is coming to light, and that the growth we are experiencing will benefit both us and others forever.

TO SAY THAT AFFLICTIONS OF LOVE RELEASE HIDDEN potential is too general a statement to be fully help-

Recognizing the Gain

ful. One who is in pain will bear that pain more easily if he or she can identify the specific areas of development in which growth is occurring.

Afflictions of love can deepen our attachment to G-d. There is an innate human desire to feel independent and capable of running one's own life. That desire, however, blocks our recognition of G-d, for to recognize G-d is to recognize our dependence upon Him.

Only with the greatest reluctance do we surrender our sense of control. When confronted with difficulties, we instinctively seize upon any possible solution that does not force us to turn to G-d or admit that we need Him. Intense suffering forces upon us an awareness of how many of the external events affecting our lives are beyond our control. At that point, we are left with no choice but to turn towards G-d.

Suffering further forces us to clarify the nature of our connection to G-d. As long as our lives are pretty much running according to plan, we have little incentive to reflect with any depth upon the nature of our connection to G-d. Suffering can help us go beyond viewing G-d as an abstract idea. In the throes of suffering, we sense G-d's nearness.

The halachah is that if one is in the presence of a sick person, he may pray for him in Aramaic (*Yoreh Deah* 335:3). While one may generally not pray privately in Aramaic, since the angels do not understand that language and cannot help "carry" the prayers to G-d, this case is different — since G-d Himself stands in the presence of the sick. No intermediary is needed, for the prayers go directly to Him. One message comes through very clearly: In times of suffering, G-d is very close. Suffering significantly reduces our absorption with the physical world. As physical pleasures hold less allure, we become more keenly aware of G-d's immediate presence in our lives.

In addition to developing our relationship with G-d, suffering has the power to develop deeper sensitivities. Until we have experienced the loss of a dear one, we do not fully appreciate the value of life. Until we have known pain ourselves, we are less able to truly feel the pain of others. Until we ourselves have gone through the full spectrum of emotions that inevitably accompany personal tragedy, we cannot fully appreciate what others are going through. If one possesses any ability to get outside of himself, suffering will deepen his ability to understand and connect to others.

Finally (and here I will be brief because this strikes a very personal chord) afflictions of love can force us to redefine the meaning of our lives. Confronted with extreme pain, or the anticipation of such pain, a person may experience the feeling that life is simply no longer worth the suffering that it now entails. He or she is forced to ask, "Is it possible to redefine life — my life — in a way that makes it worth the pain or anxiety?" In the process, he is forced to see the world in a far sharper perspective than previously.

Suffering may also serve as a reality check. When things are going well, we tend to have exaggerated ideas about our commitment to G-d and the extent of our spiritual development. As long as life is going along smoothly, it is easy to believe in a benevolent G-d. Only when adversity tests our belief and commitment do we ascertain the true nature of our commitment. Sometimes G-d provides us with a spiritual mirror in order to motivate us to strengthen that which is weaker than we suspect.

Other times our misconceptions about our own spiritual standing cause us to look at our neighbor with a jaundiced eye. We may feel G-d has been more generous with him than with us, despite the fact that we are more worthy of G-d's beneficence.

When we start thinking that way, we challenge G-d to reveal that our spiritual level is not necessarily so great as we think.

Remember how Satan brought about the suffering of Job. He claimed that Job was not the great *tzaddik* that he appeared to be. "His devotion is only the result of his wealth and success. Take those away, and he'll curse you," Satan told G-d. As a result Job was tested in ways that have become synonymous with suffering. Once the question of his faith had been raised, it had to be answered. When we compare ourselves to others, on the grounds that we are more righteous than they and therefore deserve more of G-d's bounty, we invite G-d to test us as He tested Job.

Even where we do not compare ourselves to others, we may invite such tests by virtue of our confidence in our own spiritual attainments. The result can be humiliating. A person whose life has focused around spiritual pursuits may have an exaggerated sense of his own spiritual level until one day his life begins to unravel. At that point, he may suddenly realize that his faith is shallow, his commitment shaky.

Until we are pushed by adversity, we are not forced to internalize our ideals. Suffering, then, serves as a needed corrective for our exalted vision of ourselves, and challenges us to make that vision a reality.

7
THE SUFFERER AS A MODEL

NOT EVERYTHING THAT HAPPENS TO US IS FOR OUR OWN personal development. Our suffering may be for the benefit of others as well. Sometimes G-d sends us difficulties not because we need to remove the effects of our transgressions or to reveal hidden potential but rather because of the inspiration and strength our example can provide to those around us. That is a third possible reason for suffering.

When hardship strikes, the one suffering naturally asks, "If G-d exists and is all-powerful why has He created this difficult situation? Why doesn't He help?" G-d is far away, while the pain is immediate.

Dedication to G-d can falter under this pressure. Who needs the extra responsibilities of a religion that seems so out of touch with the reality of one's world? Let's say, however, that someone sees me enduring my own terrible suffering with my faith intact — he receives the most powerful message possible that G-d exists. If I do not abandon my faith in G-d, despite my personal tragedy, I become a role model of *emunah* (belief).

When we refer to Avraham, Yitzchak, and Yaakov as the Fathers, and Sarah, Rivkah, Rachel, and Leah as the Mothers, we mean this in many senses. One is that they are role models. They show us how to maintain and develop our dedication to G-d through adversity.

But our patriarchs and matriarchs do not merely serve as a source of inspiration. They also expanded our capacities. Their spiritual strength became a legacy for their descendants. Though Jean Baptiste Lamarck's theory that acquired physical traits can be transmitted to offspring has been conclusively refuted, a Lamarckian transmission does apply in the spiritual realm. The spiritual achievements of previous generations create new spiritual capacities that subsequent generations draw upon. Our ability to withstand the challenges in our own lives stems from the strength that our patriarchs and matriarchs developed within themselves. Today, as well, individuals may be selected by G-d to experience extreme adversity in order to strengthen the rest of us, not only by their example, but by creating new reserves of human character for future generations.

Both Avraham and Yitzchak accepted G-d's command that Yitzchak be sacrificed. Why is this constantly held up as the ultimate act of self-sacrifice? After all, Jewish history is replete with accounts of simple folk giving up their lives and those of their children for the sanctification of G-d's name. The answer is that Avraham and Yitzchak created the reservoir of capacity for self-sacrifice that has sustained the Jewish people throughout our history. But for the binding of Isaac, subsequent generations could not have made the sacrifices they did. This principle is well illustrated by a familiar story. The *Midrash* (*Eichah Rabbah* 1:50) recounts the confrontation between a Jewish woman named Miriam, her seven sons, and a foreign ruler.[1] The ruler orders the sons, starting with the oldest, to bow down to an idol. Each one refuses, citing a different Biblical verse prohibiting idol worship, and is put to death.

The ruler is humiliated by the resolve of the sons and his inability to bend them to his will. To save face, he offers the youngest son, a boy of no more than two or three, a subterfuge that will not require actual idol worship. He will drop his signet ring in front of the idol, and the boy need do nothing more than pick it up. But even this offer is refused.

As the little boy is about to be led away to be executed, his mother takes him in her arms and tells him, "Go to Avraham, your father, and tell him for me, 'You

---

1. Josephus identifies the woman as Chanah, and that is the name by which she is most frequently known. He also identifies the foreign ruler as Antiochus, the Seleucid emperor against whom the Maccabees revolted. The Talmud (*Gittin* 57b) relates almost the identical events, without mentioning the name of the ruler or of the mother.

built one altar; I built seven. In the end, you did not sacrifice your son; I sacrificed seven.'"

The mother's statement is puzzling. At a moment of such heartbreak, did she really have nothing else to worry about other than bragging rights over Avraham?

Of course not. The mother was not telling Avraham that she was greater than he. Her message to him was: Because of what you did thousands of years ago, when you offered your beloved son Yitzchak, a simple Jewish woman would one day find the strength to offer seven sons in a single day. You planted an eternal capacity for *mesiras nefesh* (self-sacrifice) in the Jewish people.

Not only did Avraham's binding of Yitzchak have an impact upon all subsequent history, so too did Sarah's reaction. A *Midrash* (*Midrash Tanchuma Vayeira* 23) relates that after Avraham had success-fully passed G-d's test by binding Yitzchak on an alter, Satan felt deeply frustrated. He had tried very hard to prevent Avraham from offering up Yitzchak in the first place. Having failed to achieve that goal, he tried to strike at Avraham through Sarah. He told Sarah the story of what had happened, but in such a slow and drawn-out fashion that she burst into tears and died before she heard that Yitzchak was still alive.

This *Midrash* is usually understood to mean that Sarah died of grief. *Eliyahu Rabbah* (*Orach Chaim* 509:1), however, states that the sounds of the shofar on Rosh Hashanah imitate weeping to remind G-d of the tears of Sarah. That *Midrash* suggests another interpretation of Sarah's tears. What is the connection between Sarah's tears and the judgment of Rosh Hashanah? Why is it so important on that day to remind G-d of her torment at Satan's hands?

The tears which Sarah shed as she listened to Satan were not just tears of grief. Sarah knew that Avraham's life would be the foundation for all of Jewish history. He was confronted with ten terrible tests *because of* — not in spite of — his righteousness. Those tests allowed him to grow spiritually. Avraham's growth, however, was not merely personal. He provided his descendents with the spiritual wherewithal to survive the tortures that history had in store for them.

If Avraham had to offer up his son, Sarah reasoned, it must be that the Jews would face similar sacrifices in the future. And thus she wept. She wept not because of her own pain, or because of concern for her husband, but rather for the pain of her future descendants. Her tears were a prayer to G-d to spare her progeny.

Thus we remember those tears on Rosh Hashanah when G-d determines what the coming year holds in store for us. We stand before Him asking for another chance to be His servants, to be given the opportunity to withstand His tests. Through the shofar we remind G-d of Sarah's tears, hoping that in the memory of those tears He will be merciful in determining the nature of those tests.[2]

---

2. The following story provides another illustration of how one's actions can transform the spiritual universe. Rabbi Yosef Karo, author of the *Shulchan Aruch*, the most important codification of Jewish law since Maimonides' *Mishneh Torah*, wrote a whole diary of his conversations with an angel who would frequently visit him. Once Rabbi Karo struggled for many days until

One who is selected by G-d to be a role model or to add to the spiritual reservoirs of the Jewish people will not have an easy life. He will be faced with extremely difficult situations, which are not a consequence of any wrongdoing on his part. By pushing the world forward in a way which goes beyond his individual responsibilities, he becomes a partner with G-d in the creation. Such a person's reward, Rabbi Moshe Chaim Luzzato tells us, is beyond description.

We have now covered three basic reasons for suffering: punishment designed to erase blockages within us created by our sins, afflictions of love that help us develop the potential within ourselves, and suffering through which one becomes a role model or increases the spiritual potential of the Jewish people. It is important to recognize than none of these reasons necessarily excludes the other. Suffering may simultaneously remove spiritual blockages and actualize hidden capacities. He may even grow to the point where he serves as a role model for others faced with tragedy. Thus a person should not despair even in the face of prolonged and severe suffering. Even if his suffering begins as a corrective for past misdeeds, at some point, it might take on an entirely different purpose, and become the means of building his *Olam Haba* and that of thousands of other Jews.

---

he finally understood a particular *mishnah*. Shortly thereafter, he heard a young child reviewing *mishnayos*, and the child explained that *mishnah* in precisely the same way Rabbi Karo had after hours of hard work. Rabbi Karo was astounded that a young child had been able to understand the *mishnah* so effortlessly, and asked his angel how that could possibly be. The angel told him that the child had only been able to understand the *mishnah* because Rabbi Karo had first brought the explanation into the world. After that, his understanding was available to everyone.

8 WHY DO THE RIGHTEOUS SUFFER?

E HAVE EXPLAINED THAT G-D CREATED THE WORLD IN order to give as much as possible to His creation.

A Communal Enterprise

The greatest gift requires that the recipient earn his reward, for only then can he can fully savor what he receives. Through the exercise of his free will, man earns the good which G-d grants. In so doing he plays a pivotal role in the realization of G-d's purpose for creation.

Many large undertakings are collective efforts. For example, the building of a shopping mall requires many different types of workers — architects, contractors, masons, plumbers, carpenters, electricians. Only if each does his specific job can the project be completed. So, too, a variety of individuals, each doing his specific task, is required, if mankind is to earn G-d's good to its fullest measure.

G-d has a vast array of good to give. No single individual can earn every type because each kind of reward is a payment for a specific good that we do. The nature of the good received is appropriate to the action and circumstances through which it was earned. A wealthy man who overcomes his greed and gives charity generously, for instance, receives a different reward than the poor man who rejoices in his portion in life.

Each one of us encounters unique tests. If we pass the test successfully, we merit the appropriate good. Only through the sum total of all of our choices can mankind as a whole earn the entire array of good which G-d intends to bestow, and thereby justify Creation in the fullest sense.

All mankind, then, is bound together in pursuit of a single goal that can only be achieved by mankind as a whole. That union is greater than the sum total of its parts. We can look to the laws of *tumah* (impurity) for an illustration of the concept that when two things are united in a common goal, they become greater than the sum of the two alone. If one blade of a pair of scissors comes in contact with *tumah*, that blade becomes impure. The other blade, which did not touch the impure object, does not become impure even though the two blades are joined. But if the scissors are being used when the blade touches the impure object, both blades become impure. Since the two blades are working together toward a common goal at the time of defilement, they have a single collective identity; they are not *two* blades, but *one* pair of scissors. When we work together to realize the goal of Creation, we too constitute a union that is greater than the sum of its parts.

Now let us put this in a human context. Let us say that a group of us teams up to paint a picture. (That, in fact, is how many of the old masters used to paint. Teams of students and apprentices assisted in the production of a single painting.) My job is to apply a single dab of white paint to the canvas. That is all I do. But when the picture is finished and that spot appears in a stunning portrait as the glint in the eye of a proud aristocrat, the significance and value of my small act has been greatly magnified by being part of a larger whole.

G-d set up Creation as a collective project. Each of us functions not just as an individual but within a larger framework. When our actions are evaluated not as isolated acts but within the larger context of a collective undertaking, their significance is magnified and our rewards correspondingly greater.

Even if we lack the capacity to make a grand contribution, G-d, in His kindness, evaluates our contributions in the context of the larger whole. What would that portrait look like without the glint in the eye? As long as we make ourselves part of the project by aligning ourselves philosophically with those directing the enterprise, and support their efforts, we receive a reward far greater than our actual investment of time and energy would merit.

RECOGNITION THAT THE JEWISH PEOPLE CONSTITUTES A collective entity provides us with the key to under-

Part of a Larger Whole

standing the role of the *tzaddik,* the righteous person. Together we form a single body; each of us is a limb of the collective body. A change in one limb can affect the whole. When a person smokes and clogs up his lungs not only do his lungs suffer; his whole body is weakened, and it becomes difficult to even walk around the block. The opposite is also true. If he succeeds in breaking his habit not only his lungs benefit; his whole body is rejuvenated.

Similarly, when an individual or group of individuals is unusually dedicated to G-d, everyone gains. All those who respect and support the *tzaddik,* and connect themselves to the enterprise of which he is part, achieve a closeness to G-d far beyond what they might achieve individually.

Because of his communal role the *tzaddik* sometimes faces challenges which he would never have been given as a private individual. He does not need to be punished to remove the effects of transgression. He has already developed his potential and reached exceptional spiritual heights. Yet he may still be confronted with challenges that will test him beyond what could reasonably be demanded of him as an individual — all in order to benefit the entire community.

Let me illustrate this. When a person goes blind, he needs to develop his hearing to compensate for the loss of his sight. His hearing might have been perfectly adequate before he went blind, but now that he has lost his sight, he needs to gather much more information through hearing. His ears must bear more of the burden of orienting him to the surrounding world. Similarly, someone suffering from a crippling illness must be much more efficient in the management of his time and energy, due to the limits on both. He must rely on his mind to compensate for the shortcomings of his body.

As with the individual, so it is with society. When others lose their ability to come close to G-d, the *tzaddik* is called upon to take up the slack that exists in society and come even closer to G-d. By doing so, he lifts the entire community. His suffering forces him to dig even deeper within himself to further improve the quality of his relationship with G-d.

When things are going fine it is easy to pray to G-d. We need not pay much attention. "Life is great; thank You, G-d," we say, and go merrily on our way. But when things are difficult, we do not talk to G-d so casually. Our faith that He runs the world and has reasons for His actions must become rock hard. Under pressure, our faith cannot remain in a state of inertia. Either we move closer to G-d or we break away entirely. When the *tzaddik* is pressed to the wall, he moves even closer to G-d. He asks himself, "Why am I suffering? What have I done wrong? What needs correction? Have I been lax in realizing my potential?"

Though he will grow personally as a consequence of his suffering, the faults or needs of the *tzaddik* are not necessarily the cause of his suffering. He is already doing enough to ensure his own personal redemption. Nevertheless he is called upon to raise the overall level of the collective.

That is not the same as being a role model. As a role model, the *tzaddik* suffers to set an example for others. The changes *they* make as a result of his example are the goal of his suffering. Here, the change in the *tzaddik himself* is the essential factor. His growth affects the whole by virtue of his being part of that whole.

The *Midrash* explains the suffering of the righteous with an analogy: A farmer has a large field to plow, seed, and harvest. He has two oxen, one healthy and strong, the other sickly and weak. The farmer puts the yoke on the strong ox to work the major expanse of the field while the weak one does the border areas. Both will ultimately eat from the harvest.

The farmer is G-d; the field is the world. G-d wants His world worked, so that He can harvest it. Not everyone can make the same kind of contribution, but the work, ultimately, must all be done. The greater burden falls on those who are capable of carrying it — i.e., the righteous — even though the project is a joint one for the benefit of all.

We refer to this dependence upon the *tzaddik* three times daily in the weekday *Shemoneh Esrei* prayer. The blessing "*al hatzaddikim v'al hachassidim,* on the righteous and on the devout" invokes G-d's mercy upon all of us. The blessing begins by enumerating several classes of praiseworthy people. Heading the list of those for whom we ask G-d's mercy are the righteous (*tzaddikim*) and the pious. We acknowledge that the righteous deserve G-d's mercy and call upon Him to show them that mercy. Then we pray that we too will be included within the framework of the divine bounty showered on the *tzaddik*. Though we ourselves might not merit His mercy, we pray that by supporting the *tzaddikim* and what they stand for, we will share in that goodness which G-d has in store for them.

This collective relationship allows the *tzaddik* to act not merely for his *own* good, but for the good of *all*. It creates an opportunity for him to give to the world. Thus the Talmud (*Berachos* 17b) tells us that the entire world was sustained because of R' Chanina ben Dosa. He himself received nothing in this world and was known for his abject poverty; a bushel of carobs each week was sufficient for his needs. Though he brought blessing to the entire world, he himself took nothing. His work was for others. Rabbi Moshe Chaim Luzzato points out that the righteous bear their increased responsibilities not only for the good of the world, but also to "do good to G-d," as it were. For G-d was motivated to create the world out of a desire to give, and the *tzaddik* allows Him to do that by increasing society's overall capacity to receive.

BECAUSE THE *TZADDIK* IS THE STRONGEST AND MOST RELIABLE element in the collective body, he may be called upon

Withstanding the Pain

to suffer in order to bring the larger community closer to G-d. In addition, his personal suffering may also be a means to rid mankind or his community of the filth of transgression that has crept into their lives. This is punishment, but not punishment of an individual. Punishment need not be meted out solely on an individual basis. Punishment may be a corrective for the collective as a whole.

Here, too, the *tzaddik* plays a special role. Just as he possesses the strength to bring the world closer to G-d, so does he have the strength to withstand the painful cleansing process required to clear blockages that have formed through our collective shortcomings.

When poison has been introduced into the system, it must be removed. Sometimes the process of removing the blockage is unpleasant, even painful, but the alternative is worse. Not all organs and limbs of the body always survive the curative process intact. Often poison is drained from the strongest part of the body and the overall level of the poison in the body as a whole drops.

If the *tzaddik* is the one who suffers, he will surely be cleansed in the process and he may simultaneously grow in character or act as a role model. But the direct cause for his suffering need not be personal. His suffering is on our behalf. He takes the cleansing purgative on behalf of all, and in the process the poisons are drained from the collective body. Our literature refers to such suffering as the atonement for his generation.

Let us say a *tzaddik* lives in a particularly materialistic or hedonistic culture, in which the pursuit of physical pleasures and material goods is the prime focus of life. Though he will be the least tainted by the pursuit of such things, everyone is touched to some degree. The *tzaddik* might then be afflicted with a debilitating personal illness, or have a close relative who is thus afflicted. That experience leads him to a deeper recognition that true satisfaction does not lie in the pleasures of this world, and a redoubled dedication to service of G-d. The degree to which he removes himself from the distractions of this world has an impact upon the whole community. That impact is not limited to the example he sets. Because the *tzaddik* is part of the larger whole, his personal change transforms the whole.

We will talk about the Holocaust in more detail later. But this idea of the *tzaddik* suffering for the whole helps us understand why so many righteous people suffered so grievously during that period. A number of great men said that they understood that what was happening to them was not judgment for their personal misdeeds, but was rather part of a collective process. They saw themselves as the strong part of the body of the Jewish people, the part which was capable of absorbing the needed pain for the benefit of all.

There are many stories of teachers gathering their students on the verge of their slaughter to strengthen their resolve and to explain the Heavenly decree upon them. When the Nazis and their eager Lithuanian collaborators gathered the men of Kelm for mass extermination, Rabbi Daniel Movshowitz, the head of the yeshiva, requested a few minutes to address his students before the slaughter began. The commanding officer agreed.

Reb Daniel quoted the *piyut* recited on Yom Kippur that recounts how the angels themselves cried out upon seeing Rabbi Akiva's flesh raked by metal combs, "This is Torah, and this is its reward?" Hashem replied, "If I hear another word, I'll return the world to the primordial void."

At that moment, Reb Daniel explained, the world had lost any merit to justify its continued existence. Yet Hashem had promised not to bring another Flood, wiping out all of mankind, and so had chosen the Ten Martyrs mentioned in the *piyut* as an atonement for the rest of the world. If the angels forced Hashem to restrain His hand and to spare the Ten Martyrs, they would, in effect, force G-d to destroy a world no longer worthy of existence.

Turning to his students, Reb Daniel told them that they stood at that moment in exactly the same position as the Ten Martyrs: The world had lost the merit to exist. Only through the atonement of their deaths would Hashem stay His hand and not return it to the primordial void. Therefore, he urged his students, "Let us be neither confused nor frightened, but rather let us accept upon ourselves this awesome responsibility with love."

With that he turned to the chief of the murderers and told him, "I have finished. Now you can begin."[1]

Such suffering by the righteous in turn places a tremendous responsibility upon each of us. The right-

---

1. Rabbi Elchonon Wasserman, who returned to Europe from America in order to join his students in almost certain death, addressed his students in a similar fashion just prior to their execution in the Kovno ghetto. See Appendix.

eous give so much, often their very lives, in order that we should survive. Hence it is incumbent upon us to make something significant of our lives to make their sacrifice meaningful.

UNTIL NOW, WE HAVE SAID THE SUFFERING OF THE *TZADDIK* affects the collective body because he is a part of the whole. When he suffers and grows, the whole grows together with him. A change in the *tzaddik* touches upon all the other parts of the collective body.

Learning Our Lesson

The *tzaddik* also affects the community on a more indirect level. We have already discussed that G-d may bring suffering into our lives so that we might act as role models for others. By virtue of their remarkable character and accomplishments, the righteous are particularly powerful examples for us. Indeed providing a model for others is one of their primary purposes in life.

One of the obstacles which human nature presents to spiritual growth, however, is that we quickly become accustomed to those things which we see often, even when they are exceptional in nature. If we live in proximity to a *tzaddik,* we unfortunately begin to take him for granted and his example loses its power to influence us.

Sometimes G-d takes a *tzaddik* from this world to trigger within us a new appreciation of his greatness. The sudden heightened awareness of what was lost to the world may inspire in us a powerful impulse to emulate him and to integrate the lessons of his life into ours. Thus the Sages state, "*Gedolim tzaddikim bemisasan yoser mebechayeihen,* the righteous are greater in their death than in their life" (*Chullin* 7b). The righteous often sacrifice their lives in order to bring the nation closer to G-d. They are willing to give up their lives, if that is the only way to cause the generation to take heed of their example.

WHEN A *TZADDIK* DIES, HIS GENERATION BECOMES MORE profoundly aware of his life and character. To the extent

A Reason to Die

others are inspired to emulate him, his death contributes to the future of the Jewish people. In addition, there are circumstances under which the *tzaddik* realizes that his continued existence harms the nation and therefore prays for death.

The Jewish people cannot grow spiritually and accomplish its historical task without proper role models and leaders. An impoverished generation, lacking leaders, cannot be held accountable for its lowly state. On the other hand, there can be no stronger indictment of a generation than the fact that it has ignored the great *tzaddikim* in its midst. When this happens, the righteous may prefer death to serving, even indirectly, as a reproach to the Jewish people.

Moses is the classic example. After the Jews departed from Sinai, on what was to have been the final stage in their journey to the Land of Israel, they complained about the *manna* and the restrictiveness of Torah Law. G-d became very angry with them. At that point, Moses begged G-d to do away with him (*Numbers* 11:4-15). Moses suspected that the Children of Israel were being judged according to a strict standard precisely because so much more could be expected of a generation with Moses as its leader. Moses was prepared to die in order that G-d not judge His people harshly.

The book of Yonah provides another example of a righteous man who chose to die rather than bring harm to his people. G-d told Yonah to go to Nineveh, a gentile city, and rebuke them for their transgressions. He was instructed to tell the inhabitants that if they did not repent in forty days the city would be destroyed. Instead of obeying G-d's command, Yonah ran away. He knew that the people of Nineveh would heed his warning and turn from their evil ways. Their repentance would then stand as an indictment of the Jewish people, who had not repented in the face of all the prophetic warnings they had received.

Jews often demonstrate a deep-rooted stubbornness about changing their behavior. Not for nothing did G-d characterize us as a "stiff-necked people." Yonah feared that the contrast between the stiff-necked behavior of the Jews and the repentance of gentiles would make the Jewish people look even worse in G-d's eyes. So Yonah ran away rather than deliver his prophecy. He knew that the Divine punishment for suppressing one's prophecy is death, and yet he did so to protect his fellow Jews.

MOSES AND YONAH UNDERSTOOD THAT AS LEADERS THEIR lives were only for the sake of the Jewish people.

The *Tzaddik's* Responsibility

There is another dimension that we should not ignore. Our lives are only for the purpose of bringing the world to the ultimate perfection which G-d intended. To do so requires the entire Jewish nation, not just a collection of individuals, no matter how distinguished those individuals may be. Our relationship with G-d cannot be separated from His relationship to the Jewish people as a whole. The righteous, however, are more conscious of this interrelationship than most of us. As a consequence, they are willing to make the requisite sacrifices.

The righteous exist for the sake of the collective whole. The potential for greatness with which G-d imbues them is in direct correlation to the needs of the nation. When Moses was on Mount Sinai receiving the Torah, the Jews built the Golden Calf and began to worship it. G-d demanded that Moses descend immediately, as if to say, "You were only brought up to this level of greatness for the sake of the people. Now that they are no longer worthy, you must go down."

Since great men are only given their capabilities for the sake of their generation, they are also held accountable if they fail to provide their generation with the leadership and models it requires. Not using one's potential or failing to fulfill one's task can also lead to Divine punishment.

We often make the mistake of viewing our lives as ours by right — as something that can be taken away only for gross misconduct. That is a fundamental mistake. Life is a gift. Only when we use the talents and capabilities which were given to us do we fully merit that gift.

When a righteous man sees a general failing in his generation, he has no permission to ignore it, or to solace himself that he has not personally stumbled in the same manner as his contemporaries. In Yiddish, we refer to a righteous man who keeps to the sidelines and does not involve himself with the matters of his generation as a *tzaddik in pelts* — a righteous man bundled up in a fur coat. Just as a wealthy person wrapped in a warm fur coat can easily forget the less fortunate shivering in the cold, so too the *tzaddik in pelts* is oblivious to the spiritual depravation around him.

Since a *tzaddik's* whole purpose is to uplift his generation, he cannot excuse himself from trying to change others or from otherwise involving himself on the grounds of modesty. That is false modesty. Modesty, in Jewish terms, means dedicating all one's abilities to G-d, not denying that one possesses any such abilities. Granted that task of changing one's generation may seem hopeless. But that is not our calculation. Our job is to make the effort required of us and leave the results to G-d. Our actions are not the direct cause of what happens in the world. Rather they are the pipelines through which G-d brings His blessing to the world or retracts it.

All Jewish history is an unbroken saga of survival against impossible odds. To despair of success, then, is to willfully forget all the good G-d has done for us in the past. And if we don't make the effort required of us, we show that we are not really bothered with the alienation of our fellow Jews from G-d. For that lack of concern, even the greatest *tzaddik* can be held accountable.

The *tzaddik* exists in order to lead his generation away from sin, and he is responsible for all those transgressions that were in his power to prevent. Accordingly, he may often be the first one punished for the sins of his generation, even though he is only implicated by virtue of failing to prevent them.

Aharon exemplifies this responsibility of the *tzaddik*. The worship of the Golden Calf was a most disastrous event in Jewish history. It permanently altered the nature of the relationship between Israel and G-d. All punishments which befall the Jewish people throughout history, say our Sages, are installments on the payment for that transgression, even though only a small minority of the people worshipped the Golden Calf. Aharon himself did not participate in that worship, and yet he is held accountable for not having prevented it. All the sacrifices he brought at the time of his investment as High Priest were atonement for the sin of the Golden Calf.

It is a great gift to be part of the larger organic whole of the Jewish people. For as we have said, the significance of any positive act is greatly magnified. But this also places additional responsibilities upon us. Because we are a part of a whole we have both the capacity and the obligation to help our fellow man fulfill *mitzvos* and to keep him away from transgression. We cannot confine ourselves to our own *daled amos* — the four cubits of our own private space — for we are part of a larger entity. Nor can we accomplish what we are supposed to accomplish as individuals. That requires the whole Jewish people.

All that we have said concerning the interdependence of the Jewish people applies with particular force to the *tzaddikim*. They have been given unusual capabilities, and with those heightened capabilities go greater responsibilities. The righteous are granted their gifts for the sake of the community. As a consequence, the *tzaddik's* public and communal self overshadows his private self. The righteous live for the community, and at times, they may even be called upon to die for the community or to bear a burden of suffering on behalf of the community.

For that reason, their suffering constitutes a category unto itself.

9
WHY DO
CHILDREN SUFFER?

OMETIMES ALL THE EXPLANATIONS FOR SUFFERING THAT we have offered ring hollow. In particular, that is true with respect to the pain of children born with severe handicaps or illnesses, thereby condemned to live lives of constant suffering. These children have done nothing to deserve their fate. Even when their sickness or suffering arises later in childhood, it cannot be attributed to punishment, for we are not held accountable for our actions in Heaven until the age of twenty.

Though it is humbling to see what heights many such children reach, the concept of *yisurim shel ahavah*, pains of love, which are meant to enhance growth, does not apply to many of them. Though we cannot know, for instance, what kind of inner development severely brain-damaged children experience, it is hard to accept that their disabilities foster some significant growth in them as individuals. No doubt many such children stimulate tremendous growth in their parents and siblings, summoning forth from them new levels of *chesed*. Yet why should the children themselves suffer so that their loved ones can grow?

Nor can we claim that suffering children have been appointed to purify and raise the generation as a whole. That status is reserved for *tzaddikim*, who have developed themselves until they are capable of bearing such a burden. What opportunity have these children had to make themselves into *tzaddikim*?

There are many other instances where suffering cannot be explained according to the categories we have established. The suffering of children merely presents the problem most starkly because there are no unknown factors which could possibly explain that suffering.

IN THE FRAMEWORK WE HAVE OUTLINED UNTIL NOW, THE individual is basically responsible for his actions. *He*

Gilgul Neshamos

transgressed; *he* is punished for that transgression. A man has the potential to reach a certain point; *he* is pushed to reach that point. That framework cannot encompass the children we are discussing.

To comprehend the plight of such children, we must broaden our understanding to encompass the concept of *gilgul neshamos*, the transmigration of souls.[1] As *gilgul neshamos* belongs to the esoteric doctrines of *kabbalah*, our discussion will of necessity be very limited. Yet without the framework of *gilgul neshamos*, there are tragedies that simply defy any understanding.

Briefly, the doctrine of *gilgul neshamos* declares that souls may return to the world many times in different bodies. Every soul comes into the world with a particular mission and the ability to accomplish it. But that potential can only be actualized through the body. Through the exercise of our free will, we either realize our spiritual potential or negate it. When we exercise our free will in accord with the yearnings of our soul, the body and soul are united.

Our goal in life is to give the fullest expression to our souls by acting in accord with our soul's aspirations. No one succeeds in doing so all the time. That being the case, our soul has not yet fulfilled the mission for which it was sent to earth. Thus souls are sent back to this world again and again until they fully express themselves.

The concept of *gilgul neshamos* is directly relevant to our discussion, and provides the key to understanding otherwise inexplicable tragedies. A child is born, G-d forbid, with a severe disability and dies

---

1. Transmigration of souls is more generally associated with Eastern mysticism than with Torah Judaism, and many are shocked to find that it is based on classical Jewish sources. Yet *gilgul neshamos* is discussed in the *Zohar* and the works of Nachmanides. Rabbi Moshe Chaim Luzzato even finds the doctrine hinted at in the *siddur*.

shortly thereafter. What possible purpose could have been served by that brief life? True, the child's parents become greatly attached to him, and his passing may leave them with an enhanced sensitivity to life. But how does that explain things from the perspective of the child? Where did he have an opportunity to confront the challenges of life, to choose to act in a certain way or not?

If we accept the possibility of *gilgul*, or reincarnation, we can begin to make sense of the child's life. Let us say his soul belonged previously to an individual of a generally good character but who lacked a full appreciation of the gift of life. That is all he was missing. In order to gain that appreciation, he does not need to relive a full life. It is sufficient that he return and teach his parents how much there is to be grateful for in just being alive. With that small contribution, his soul has completed its task and is free to return to a higher place.

The *Chazon Ish*, one of the greatest men of his generation, would stand up for retarded children. He reasoned that if this soul has been placed in a body with limited capacities, it must already be a very elevated soul, with only a very little left to accomplish before completing its journey in the world.

WE WERE FORCED TO INTRODUCE THE CONCEPT OF *GILGUL neshamos* because of the problem created by the birth

Broader Implications

of children born with severe defects and other forms of childhood suffering. But once introduced, it is obvious that the general principle cannot be limited to just those whose entire life is otherwise inexplicable. It also has reference to our own lives. Our lives too are affected by our soul's unfinished business.

The idea of reincarnation is deeply unsettling. It provokes many questions: What is my relationship to those people in whose body my soul previously dwelled? Why am I accountable for their choices? If we share the same soul are we the same person, or are we both part of a meta-person? If the choices of a previous incarnation are not mine, how can they bind me in any way?

What emerges from the concept of *gilgul neshamos* is that our souls only return to earth because of something left undone the previous time around. All our social and familial circumstances have been chosen by G-d with precise regard to the particular task of repair still left. Still, we ask, "Why should I, in any way, be bound by what someone else did?"

That question, however, could have been asked long before we introduced the concept of *gilgul neshamos*. We all recognize that our lives are shaped to a very great degree by the circumstances into which we are born. Certainly a person cannot be blamed for being born into a dysfunctional family. Yet the nature of his family will obviously have a large impact on the person he becomes. And the same is true of a host of other life circumstances into which a person is born.

Should a person born into difficult socio-economic or familial circumstances, or who lacks gifts that others possess, refuse to work on developing himself on the grounds that he has been treated "unfairly" and others have "easier" circumstances? One can, of course, do that, and many do. But it is foolish. We have only one life, only one opportunity to live. If we let it pass us by, we lose everything.

So it is with my soul, however used or misused it was in previous lives. It is I. I am in the world to actualize my soul in the physical realm. That process is the only one that gives meaning to my life. Whether it is easy or hard makes no difference — either way it's my only life. I must accept my soul with all the baggage that it brings. That doesn't mean that I passively accept those past injuries. They are the unique challenges with which I have been presented. They define my mission in life. My soul's injuries are mine and must be healed; its health is my health. The condition in which I leave that soul vis-à-vis the condition in which I received it determines my eternity.

We must not think of the soul as a partner with whom we have been forced into a reluctant marriage. Our soul is the basis of our being; it defines us. To reject our soul is to reject ourselves. The personality with which we are born sets the parameters of our life work. But even the negative traits are only expressions of energy that has to be re-channeled.

How we meet the challenges of giving positive expression to the various traits with which we are born determines the quality of our life, for that is the true measure of how we have employed our free will. Those challenges, then, present us with the greatest opportunity for growth and for giving meaning to our lives.

THERE IS ANOTHER WAY THAT EVENTS THAT TOOK PLACE LONG before we were born can weigh heavily on our own

The Sins of the Fathers

lives. The Torah instructs us not to worship idols for, "I am the L-rd your G-d, a jealous G-d, Who visits the transgressions of the fathers upon the sons to the third and fourth generation of those who hate Me" (*Exodus* 20:5). The verse implies that a son will suffer for the transgressions of his parents, grandparents and even great-grandparents. The Talmud (*Sanhedrin* 27), however, mitigates this harsh decree, and explains the words "of those who hate Me" to mean that the children suffer for those sins only if they continue in the ways of the parents.

If the child breaks with his parents' ways he will not suffer for their transgressions. But if he continues in their path, he will be punished not only for his own actions, but for their acts as well. Why should that be the case?

When a negative trait is passed down from one generation to another it becomes ever more deeply ingrained in each succeeding generation. When the chain of transmission of a particular character trait extends back several generations, a child may grow up without ever having had a familial role model who does not possess that trait. The negative characteristic has become fully embedded in the child's character, and is therefore very difficult to uproot.

Suffering, as we have seen, is G-d's means of removing negative traits. The more deeply embedded those traits are, the greater the suffering required to remove them. The child suffers for the sins of the parents when his parents instill in him an attachment to particular negative traits. By virtue of that attachment, he needs a more severe punishment to extirpate that trait. (Psychologists today spend much time analyzing the difficulty in uprooting inherited character traits.)

But again it is pointless to ask, "Why should I be punished just because I had lousy parental role models, and my parents in turn had equally wretched models?" If someone poisoned my food, I would have to take painful and unpleasant medicine. No one in their right mind would refuse to take the medicine on the grounds that it is unfair that he should have to take unpleasant medicine because someone else poisoned his food.

With respect to the circumstances of our birth it makes no more sense to complain of the unfairness than it would for a poison victim. Such complaining is pointless. Just as the poison has to be removed or we will die, so too do we have to remove the negative character traits or suffer the consequences.

We are each born into a particular situation, with its own unique challenges. What we have to remember is that the challenges we confront have been given us by G-d so that our souls can fulfill their mission.

10

SELF-IMPOSED SUFFERING

HAT PLAGUES US MOST ABOUT SUFFERING IS THE QUESTION: Why does G-d bring pain into our lives or the lives of people we care about? Though we have suggested a number of possible explanations, Maimonides has a sobering thought on the subject of suffering: Much of the suffering we experience in this world is self-inflicted.

Maimonides is not referring to the spiritual causality we discussed earlier — i.e., that our transgressions create spiritual toxins and G-d brings suffering to cleanse us of them. Rather Maimonides is referring to a more direct causality. We eat delicious fatty foods and wake up twenty years later with severely clogged arteries; we lead highly stressful lives without exercise until we suffer our first heart attack; we smoke cigarettes until we eventually develop lung cancer or any other of the host of problems that accompany smoking.

Today we know a lot more about how the body functions and what kinds of activities are harmful to us than we once did. But we still frequently ignore this knowledge rather than let it impede our enjoyment. Yet when the natural consequences of such actions follow, we turn to G-d and ask Him why He is subjecting us to such pain. That is childish. What happened was entirely predictable, and we have only our own recklessness to blame. When we ask G-d, "Why?" our real question is, "Why didn't You perform a miracle to protect me?"

G-d is not in the business of performing miracles to save us from our own folly. Man has free will to choose his particular path in life. Choosing a path implies choosing the results of that path. Free will is meaningless if we can choose what to do, but have no control over the consequences of our actions. If we abuse the privilege and injure ourselves, G-d does not generally step in to save us. To do so would destroy the connection between our choices and their consequences, and thereby undermine the significance of our free will. The way our tradition puts it is, "It is forbidden to have mercy on someone who lacks judgment" — i.e., "who acts without discernment."

Intelligence, or rather knowledge, is in a constant flux from man's vantage point. Science does not present a single monolithic view throughout time. What was considered harmless yesterday is found to be harmful today. Smoking was once considered an innocent indulgence. Today it is viewed as a deadly killer. The smoker of years ago acted out of ignorance, not stupidity. G-d does not withhold His mercy from the ignorant. As King David says, "*shomer pesa'im Hashem,* G-d protects the simple" (*Psalms* 116:6).

G-d's protection from our own ignorance does not contradict our free will, for we are in a realm where we have no knowledge and therefore no control. In such cases G-d tends to be indulgent. He does not demand more from us. What counts is not what we do, but rather that we act with intelligence to the best of our ability. More cannot be demanded of us than that we use our intelligence and avoid obvious dangers.

In the eighth blessing of *Shemoneh Esrei,* we pray, "*refaeinu Hashem veneirafei; hoshi'einu venivashei'a,* Heal us, Hashem, and we will be healed; save us and we will be saved." Why the double language? If "save us and we will be saved" did not also refer to matters of health, what is it doing in this blessing altogether? The Gaon of Vilna answers, "Heal us, Hashem, and we will be healed" is a request to be healed from illness. "Save us and we will be saved" is a request for protection from those things that are harmful to us, but which we do not know to be harmful. Maimonides' point about self-inflicted misery does not apply only to illness. All foolhardy behavior has natural consequences. Risky investments may lead to poverty. Walking through Central Park at night invites muggers.

Maimonides, it is true, speaks about illness. His position that we are responsible for most of our illnesses seems harsh and hard to accept. It is important to remember, however, that he still does not consider self-inflicted suffering to be meaningless. He is not saying, "You did it to yourself. So don't look for purpose." Nothing that happens to us is without purpose — i.e., completely unrelated to our relationship with G-d. All that Maimonides means is that but for our own recklessness, G-d might not have imposed a regimen of suffering. When we place ourselves in an inherently dangerous environment, we need far more merits to protect us from the dangers surrounding us. If we nevertheless place ourselves in danger, instead of challenging G-d to justify the suffering imposed upon us, we should point the accusing finger at ourselves.

Yet once that suffering befalls us, it still serves all the purposes discussed previously: It can purge our spiritual systems of toxins, provide a means of growth, allow us to become role models. It all depends how we choose to react to the situation.

THE SIGNIFICANCE OF A PERSON'S SUFFERING EVOLVES according to his response. Even when carelessness is

It All Depends on Our Response

the immediate cause of our pain, that pain still has a cleansing effect. Pain always reduces a man's attachment to the material world and opens the way for a stronger connection to his spiritual side. That is especially so if he accepts the pain and opens himself to its potential to change him.

Awareness of our own irresponsibility can act as a powerful wake-up call. For one thing, it forces us to recognize our impulsivity, our inability to forego instant gratification in light of the long-range costs. We have to confront our own superficiality and lack of self-control. Pain can force us to discover new, previously unrealized potential within ourselves. As those new capacities are revealed, we may even serve as role models for others. As our response to suffering matures, so does our benefit from that suffering.

It is our response to suffering, then, that often determines its meaning. Whether that suffering is experienced as purposeful or not depends on us. That is easily understood with respect to the suffering we bring upon ourselves. But what of the suffering caused by others, in particular that inflicted by parents on their children by virtue of their lousy parenting? Let's say a parent subscribes to the old theory that children should be seen and not heard. As a result, the child may become lonely and isolated, and his communication skills atrophy.

The hurts inflicted on children by their parents can only be explained as a necessary corrective for failings of that child's soul in a previous life. (See Chapter 9 above.) Yet it must be admitted that the recourse to the doctrine of the transmigration of souls is not emotionally satisfying. The cause of pain — i.e., the failures of others who possessed the same soul — strikes us as very remote, while the pain itself is immediate.

But even childhood suffering can be transformed into something positive. When the child grows older, he can face whatever neglect or abuse he suffered. With help, he can break long ingrained patterns and change his life. His own suffering may have left him with unique sensitivity to the pain of others. In the process of rising above the pain of his youth, he may even become a powerful example for others of the resilience of the human soul and of its capacity for change. Suffering that has its roots in the failures of others can neverthe-less have a transformative impact upon the sufferer.

Our Sages teach us that when we grow in our response to suffering, the very reason for the suffering is transformed. Our Sages call this process by which a negative experience is transformed into a creative force for good *hamtakas hadin* (the sweetening of judgment).

So FAR WE HAVE BEEN DISCUSSING THE CAUSES OF SUFFERING as if they were clearly distinct from one another.

A Combination of Causes

However, in real life, as opposed to theory, it is perfectly plausible that several causes can be combined simultaneously. A person may both need some cleansing and have untapped potential awaiting real-ization. Neither would by itself be sufficient to trigger intense suffering, but together they might do so.

Recognition that suffering can be multi-causal answers a serious question. We have seen that G-d protects those who act unwittingly — *shomer pesa'im Hashem*. Yet we find that even before the United States Surgeon-General declared smoking to be hazardous to one's health, smokers were more likely to develop lung cancer. (If that were not the case, of course, the Surgeon-General would never have recognized the danger of smoking.) Clearly ignorance of the dangers of smoking did not serve as complete protection.

Still, widespread knowledge of the dangers of smoking makes a difference in the Divine calculus. After that danger is known, if G-d intervenes and protects the smoker from the effects of his smoking, the principle of free will that we suffer the natural consequences of our actions is violated. Prior to that knowledge becoming widespread, there is no tension between G-d's protection and man's free will. That does not mean, however, that G-d will always protect someone from the consequences, for there may be good reasons that the smoker should experience some degree of suffering. Because smoking *is* inherently dangerous and G-d's intervention is required to protect us from its effects, it could be that a lower threshold of causality is required to trigger suffering than would be the case if there was no intermediary "natural" cause and the suffering came directly from G-d.

As with every case of suffering, the crucial question is not, "Why me?" but rather, "What am I going to do in this situation?" Regardless of why we suffer, it is always in our hands to make it a meaningful and positive force in our lives.

11

WHO IS IN CONTROL?

-D IS GOOD AND HE CREATED THE WORLD IN ORDER TO bestow that goodness upon His Creation. For that good to be fully expressed, however, we must make ourselves worthy. Otherwise, it is unearned bread. Since the ultimate good is a relationship with G-d, our goal is to create a self that is capable of entering into such a relationship.

That self is created through the choices we make. If we lacked the capacity to choose — i.e., were without free will — nothing we did would have any meaning, for we would be reduced to mere extensions of G-d. As such, nothing He gave us would serve His desire to do good to a being outside Himself. Choices are only meaningful if they have specific consequences. Imagine that you were painting, and no matter what color you dipped your brush into, it came out green on the canvas. Unless choosing blue results in painting blue, the choice of colors is meaningless. Similarly, free will implies a specific consequence for each choice. Were a beneficent G-d only to reward and never punish, free will would have no meaning, and we would not be able to speak of creating ourselves.

The centrality of free will to the Divine plan, however, forces us to confront a critical question: How can we be sure that G-d's ultimate purpose for the world will be realized? What guarantee do we have that humanity will collectively make the right choices and allow G-d to bring history to its desired conclusion?

We can understand why Creation must be driven by human choice if G-d's purpose for creating the world in the first place is to be fully realized. But doesn't G-d thereby risk the whole project? What guarantee is there that we will ever complete our task?

Individuals make many good choices, and some attain a level where they almost always choose correctly. But humanity as a whole also includes many who rarely choose correctly. Why should we assume that the former will ever outweigh the latter to such a degree that G-d will bring history to its desired end?

On an individual level, most of us vacillate. Some days we are better, some days worse. In general, it is two steps forward and two steps back. Progress is halting at best, and perfection seems very far away. And on a collective level, there are clearly as many bad people as good. If Creation is truly in the hands of man, how can we do anything other than rock back and forth forever?

THOUGH G-D HAS STRUCTURED CREATION IN SUCH A WAY that history is driven by the choices we make, He still

G-d's Direction

guides the process in a manner that preserves our free will. Rabbi Moshe Chaim Luzzato describes a second way in which G-d runs the world. He terms this *Hanhagas HaMazal*, the conduct of *Mazal*. *Mazal* here does not mean luck; it is derived from the Hebrew word *nazol*, which means to drip.

Hanhagas HaMazal refers, then, to G-d's direction of events from above, rather than in reaction to human actions down below. G-d views His Creation within the context of its ultimate purpose, and He makes adjustments to alter the framework within which man's choices lead Creation towards its goal. Events which are governed by *Hanhagas HaMazal* are determined by the requirement of fulfilling G-d's ultimate purpose.

A classic example of *Hanhagas HaMazal* is the Exodus from Egypt. Within the normal geopolitical framework, the Exodus from Egypt was impossible. No slave had ever escaped from Egypt. Now, miracles do not necessarily mean that free will is no longer operative. A person might deserve to be rewarded, and the reward might take the form of miracles. That was not, however, the case in Egypt. After living for 210 years in the depraved Egyptian culture, the *Zohar* teaches, the Jews had descended to the bottom rung of spiritual depravity. Had they remained a moment longer, they would have been indistinguishable from their Egyptian hosts, and thus incapable of redemption.

If the Jews were on such a low level, we must ask: Why did G-d bring them out? The Redemption could not be justified as a reward for their good deeds.

Moses himself asked the question when G-d designated him to lead his brothers out of Egypt: In what merit did the Jews deserve redemption? G-d replied: in the merit of the Torah they will receive at Sinai. In other words, they were redeemed not for what they *had done*, but for what they *would do*. G-d told Moses that the goal of creation could only be reached through the giving of the Torah. And though the Jews had sunk so low, they were the only ones capable of rising to the level of receiving the Torah. The Jews therefore had to be redeemed.

The Exodus serves as the classic example of *Hanhagas HaMazal*. G-d initiated events based on His all-encompassing vision of the goal of Creation.

Hanhagas HaMazal is not a total departure from the concepts of reward and punishment. G-d's actions are still linked to our deeds. In *Hanhagas HaMazal*, however, it is our future actions, not our past deeds, that are central. *Hanhagas HaMazal* tempers reward and punishment by taking cognizance of what will happen later. That is what we mean when we refer to G-d's mercy. G-d shows His mercy by acting leniently now in light of what we will do in the future. That does not mean ignoring a person's conduct. When a person shows no remorse or intention to change, leniency is not merciful but a threat.

REWARD AND PUNISHMENT AND *HANHAGAS HAMAZAL* function simultaneously. Sometimes one of them dominates the course of events,

The Relationship of the Two Systems

sometimes the other. The story of Elimelech and his wife Naomi provides an example of how both systems work at the same time.

Elimelech was a leader of Israel several generations before the birth of King David. Elimelech was so rich that the entire country relied upon him for sustenance in times of drought or famine. During a bitter famine, however, Elimelech fled with his wife and two sons to Moav rather than use his vast wealth to sustain the population. For that decision to flee, Elimelech was punished severely. His two sons married non-Jewish women in Moav. Elimelech lost all his money and died. Finally, his two sons died, without children. Up until this point everything proceeded according to the system of reward and punishment.

Yet Elimelech's sojourn to Moav also became a crucial step towards the coming of Messiah. The wife of one of Elimelech's sons was Ruth. After the death of her husband, Ruth refused to be separated from her mother-in-law Naomi. She accompanied Naomi back to the Land of Israel, where she converted, and married Boaz. That union resulted three generations later in King David, from whom the Messiah will ultimately come.

G-d used Elimelech's choices to fashion the future of the Jewish people — a particular path leading to King David. Man initiated the process, and G-d brought it to completion.

G-D WEAVES OUR CHOICES INTO THE ULTIMATE PLAN FOR Creation. The Talmud, for example (*Nedarim* 32a),

Triggering Events for *Hanhagas HaMazal*

asks why our ancestors deserved the harsh exile in Egypt, and offers three possible explanations. Each of those opinions perceives in Avraham's actions a slight failure of faith for someone at Avraham's exalted level. According to one opinion, Avraham erred when, after Hashem promised at the Covenant of the Pieces that his progeny would inherit the Land, he asked, "How shall I know that I am to inherit it?" (*Genesis* 15:8) (See also our discussion of this in Chapter 5).

At first glance, Avraham appears to be asking for some tangible sign that G-d will keep His promise. But that cannot be the case. For the Divine promise that Avraham's descendants would inherit the Land follows another promise: that Avraham would have children. Avraham accepted the first promise without question, despite the fact that he and Sarah were both well past childbearing age and sterile. G-d even

praised Avraham for the faith with which he responded to that promise.

So when Avraham asked, "How shall I know...?" he
was not questioning G-d's ability to fulfill His promise.
Avraham's concern was different. He knew that to merit
the Land of Israel his descendants would require total
dedication to G-d. And he was not sure that his descendants would possess that merit and deserve to keep the
Land of Israel forever. He did not question G-d, but
rather the spiritual commitment of his descendants.

Whatever the lack of faith shown by Avraham's
question, it was obviously very slight. So slight, in
fact, that two other opinions in the Talmud reject it
as a sin at all.

Avraham's error was to question G-d's ability to
control events through *Hanhagas HaMazal.* Since
G-d's plan was contingent on a permanent connection between the Jewish people and the Land of Israel,
Avraham should have acknowledged G-d's ability to
maintain that connection without requesting a sign.

One thing is clear: The severity of the punishment strikes us as radically disproportionate to
Avraham's error. The entire Jewish people spent
hundreds of years in Egypt as a consequence of
Avraham's slight mistake.

If we look at the exile in Egypt from a different
perspective, however, this difficulty vanishes. The
Jewish people needed the experience of Egypt. In
Egypt, their faith would be purified to the degree
necessary to survive the challenges of Jewish history. Exile need not be seen as a punishment for
Avraham's question. Rather it was the answer to

that question. How can you know that your descendants will be worthy? Because of the purifying experience of Egypt.

If the Egyptian exile was necessary to G-d's plan for the Jewish people, why does the Talmud go to such lengths to find a transgression to justify the exile? The answer is that man's free will is never completely excluded, even when *Hanhagas HaMazal* determines events. Free will remains a necessary ingredient for the achievement of G-d's purpose. Thus there must be a transgression that "caused" the servitude in Egypt. From one point of view, the transgression is more pretext than cause, but it still must be there. The triggering event leading to a deeper faith was a slight absence of faith. Man's participation in the events of history was thus preserved.

We find this interrelationship of *Hanhagas HaMazal* and reward and punishment not just on a national level, but also in the lives of individuals. Rabbi Yehudah HaNasi, known simply as Rebbe, suffered from excruciating pains for many years. The Talmud (*Bava Metzia* 85a) asks why such a righteous person suffered so greatly, and answers that the pains came as a result of a certain incident. Rebbe once passed a sheep on its way to slaughter. It ran and nuzzled under Rebbe's cloak, bleating. Rebbe pushed the lamb back, saying, "Go; for this you were created." That statement, concludes the Talmud, reflected a lack of sensitivity. For that insensitivity Rebbe was punished with many years of severe pain.

Rebbe was not wrong. The lamb was destined for slaughter. We are not supposed to be vegetarians. But Rebbe did not show compassion for the animal. For this he suffered for thirteen years.

The commentaries are bothered by the imbalance between Rebbe's transgression and his punishment; the punishment does not fit the "crime." The commentators answer that Rebbe's trials were part of his preparation for leading the Jewish people through one of its most difficult historical periods. That task required him to develop all his potential. The thirteen years of suffering were designed to further that goal.

But if the suffering was necessary so that Rebbe could fulfill his role as leader of the Jewish people, why does the Talmud have to search for an explanation? Once again, the answer is that G-d's intervention to bring the world to its ultimate goal can never completely exclude an element of human free will.

We can still ask, however: if the effect is so disproportionate to the cause how is the system of free will preserved? Part of the answer is that we have no real concept of the severity of our transgressions. We are so used to G-d tempering strict justice with His mercy that when we witness strict justice, untempered by mercy, the result strikes us as out of all proportion. Rebbe, however, needed to be brought to a certain level, and therefore experienced the full measure of G-d's strict justice.

If Rebbe had never done anything wrong, he could never have been punished, without suspending the system of Divine reward and punishment. Thus there must have been something to trigger Rebbe's suffering. Rebbe's lack of compassion would not have brought down upon him the full consequences of Divine Justice in the normal course of events. But when placed in the context of Jewish history, in the decisive period when the Oral Torah was on the verge of being lost, the combination of *Hanhagas HaMazal* and human free will produced Rebbe's suffering.

HANHAGAS HAMAZAL, G-D'S INTERVENTION IN THE AFFAIRS of the world, refers not only to instances of His

Suspending Justice

direct intervention. Sometimes it refers to G-d's choice not to intervene by refraining from meting out immediate justice. *Hanhagas HaMazal* can also cause G-d to suspend the normal operation of reward and punishment, even where justice demands retribution. G-d's refraining from action is a more subtle expression of *Hanhagas HaMazal*. How, we might ask, can G-d's refraining from action advance His purpose in the world?

G-d is good and He created a good world. Man was placed into that good world with the capacity to choose evil. Even the ability to choose evil was central to the goodness of the world. The capacity to choose evil does not make the world an evil place. For one thing, the evil chosen by man is checked by G-d's justice, which results in the punishment of the evildoer. That punishment is a corrective for the one who chose poorly, akin to a bitter-tasting, yet necessary, medicine.

But if punishment is a corrective or purgative, how, we may ask, can the suspension of justice be an expression of *Hanhagas HaMazal*, of G-d's influence "dripping down" into the world? How can leaving evil unpunished further G-d's purpose when it allows evil to fester like an untended wound that threatens to overwhelm the whole organism? That question is particularly pressing for us today when this aspect of *Hanhagas HaMazal* seems to be dominant. We live in an age that denies G-d's relevance or existence to an unprecedented degree, and yet enjoys a level of prosperity hitherto unknown in human history.

Let us explain with a parable. An 18-year-old asks his parents for a motorcycle for his birthday. The parents have absolutely no desire to fulfill this wish, as they would like to celebrate many more birthdays with their son. They are well aware of the dangers of motorcycles, and are no more excited about the unsavory nature of many motorcyclists, whom they do not see as positive role models for their son.

The parents refuse. The son promises to get a high-quality helmet. The parents continue to say no; the helmet does not even begin to speak to their concerns. The son goes on a hunger strike. The parents still refuse. The son announces, "Unless you give me a motorcycle, I will kill myself. Only if you give me a motorcycle is there any chance that you'll share any more birthdays with me."

What should the parents do? Their son has made the desire for the motorcycle so much a part of himself that he cannot live without it. He will get his bike. He will have a few falls, perhaps even break a few bones. And he'll get involved with people who will be negative influences in his life.

If his parents have succeeded in imbuing him with anything of value, there is a possibility that he will wake up one day and realize how empty his life is and how transitory the thrill of his motorcycle. At that point, there is a chance that he will begin to take control of his life again.

Sometimes we must be allowed to make bad choices if we are ever to understand what was wrong with those choices. If we listened to wise counsel we would arrive at the same point, but we are often incapable of hearing the voice of reason. As a consequence, we must experience the result of our bad choices.

So it often is in our relationship with G-d. True, G-d could respond every time we embark on a false path by punishing us. That might cause us to abandon for the time being our improper goals. But we could be no closer to understanding why our goals are empty or to developing an appreciation of the proper goals in life. Deferring an improper action just because the price is too high does not constitute real growth. We still want to take the false path.

Sometimes, G-d has to give us the "bike" so that we can truly taste the bitterness of our desires. Only when we do so can we begin to redefine ourselves. The route of personal experience is longer, more difficult, and often painful, but sometimes it is the only way. The one who survives that path, however, gains a real, visceral understanding of just how vacuous and destructive was his original choice. Sometimes the price is high, but that is a price that we brought upon ourselves.

WE KNOW THAT G-D INTENSIFIES THE INFLUENCE OF *Hanhagas HaMazal*, when necessary, to keep the

The Big Picture

world moving towards its goal. The Exodus from Egypt came at a time when mankind had forgotten G-d's existence, or denied His involvement in the events of history. Creation could obviously not reach its goal as long as denial of G-d was so widespread. Through *Hanhagas HaMazal*, G-d intervened and revealed Himself.

That was at the beginning of our history as a nation. Rabbi Moshe Chaim Luzzato writes that there will be another time in history when *Hanhagas HaMazal* figures so prominently: the period leading to the coming of the Messiah. As that time approaches, *Hanhagas HaMazal* will be very much in evidence. Otherwise, we would teeter back and forth for eternity, without ever reaching the goal G-d set for His creation.

We are approaching that time now. While we do not know precisely when the Messiah will arrive, by all calculations that time is close. Just as at the dawn of our history as a nation in Egypt, we are living today in a period in which G-d has been largely forgotten. Even when we are willing to grant His existence, most of us limit our consideration of Him to a few hours a week at best. The rest of the time we attach ourselves to the material world, with all its wonders and pleasures, as if it existed totally independent of the Creator. Such an approach is a form of idol worship.

G-d already redeemed us once before from idol worship with the Exodus from Egypt. At that time, His intervention took the form of Revelation. Nevertheless we have returned to a false concept of material existence independent of G-d. This time, it would seem, G-d's intervention in history will come in a different form. To cure us of our attraction to our false picture of reality, G-d is allowing us to experience it in full.

As the end of history approaches, *Hanhagas HaMazal* expresses itself through the suspension of justice on a world-wide scale. G-d stops imposing punishments that prevent us from creating a world, as it were, independent of G-d. We are free to remake our world in the image of our dreams. It is as if G-d says to us, "Build the world according to your desire; build it as big and powerful as you like. Any reality which is separate from Me will inevitably collapse because it is based on greed and arrogance. Your dream will reveal itself to be a nightmare. The bigger and stronger you build that world, the more powerfully you will experience the nightmare. Only then will you utterly reject this idol, with every aspect of your being."

DURING PERIODS OF SUCH LARGE-SCALE SUSPENSION OF justice, individuals will suffer in undeserved ways.

Painful Fallout G-d has chosen to allow evil to spread. Choices to do evil go unpunished, and as a consequence those choices multiply. That is

G-d's intention. But in the meantime many innocent people suffer terribly. They are martyrs to world history; they have been sacrificed for the sake of the world achieving its purpose, not because of anything they did or will do.

That seems unfair. But we must remember that our lives gain meaning only through the connection we achieve with G-d. Since that connection can never be fully realized in this life, our experience in this world is but the means to the relationship we will eventually have with G-d in the World to Come. The spiritual reward we experience in the World to Come compensates for our pain in this life. Innocent victims of history will be rewarded, for they are partners in moving the world towards its goal. To be a partner of G-d is the highest plane to which a human being can aspire.

Rabbi Moshe Chaim Luzzato says that it is often the greatest souls that come into the world in these times of suspended justice. Just as the righteous voluntarily accept suffering and death for the sake of their generation, these individuals suffer for the sake of moving history towards its destined conclusion. They do not necessarily choose this sacrifice, but those put in this position possess the same inner greatness as those who, under different circumstances, willingly sacrifice themselves for G-d.

Of course these victims can develop their inner potential, or become role models, through their suffering. But that is not the principal cause of their suffering. Rather suffering grows out of the need for Creation to reach a goal. And they are being sacrificed for that historical goal.

The concept of *Hanhagas HaMazal* taking the form of G-d's hiding His presence — and apparently refraining from intervening in history — is useful to understanding the Holocaust. That is not to say that it is a full or totally satisfactory explanation for an event so incomprehensible in scale and still so raw.

The Holocaust raises many issues of Divine thought, but one clear lesson does emerge: the horror that results when man cuts himself off from G-d. The Holocaust stands as a stark refutation of the Enlightenment belief in the perfectability of man by virtue of his own reason.

Germany was considered the most cultured nation in Europe, the source of much of the Western humanist tradition. Many looked to Germany as a beacon of light pointing the world from the shackles of its religious past to a bright secular future. Yet it was this culture that gave rise to the barbarism of the Third Reich. Leading German philosophers, like Martin Heidegger, willingly provided the philosophical justification for the Reich.

For some, the Holocaust made it hard to continue believing in a benevolent G-d. But by the same token, Nazi Germany dashed all hopes of a man-made utopia. Those murdered in the Holocaust gave their lives on the altar of secular humanism, and served as the ultimate refutation of that belief.

G-D CONDUCTS THE WORLD ACCORDING TO TWO SYSTEMS. The first is that of reward and punishment, in which

Conclusion

the primary moving force of history is G-d's reactions to our choices, for good or bad. The second is the system of *Hanhagas HaMazal,* in which G-d is gently nudging the world in the right direction towards its ultimate destination. Sometimes the approach of reward and punishment is primary, sometimes *Hanhagas HaMazal* is primary. *Hanhagas HaMazal* can express itself either through direct intervention or through G-d's apparent withdrawal and hiddenness. These two systems are not exclusive. At any given point, one or another may dominate, but they are both taking place simultaneously. The two systems are enmeshed with one another in a fashion too complicated to describe in anything more than the broadest outlines.

No matter how the affairs of the world are conducted, suffering plays a crucial role; it is always meaningful and purposeful. Even the apparent anarchy of the Holocaust, which claimed the righteous and the less righteous together, was part of the larger pattern of purpose.

12

ACKNOWLEDGING OUR EMOTIONAL REALITY

E HAVE SKETCHED AN INTELLECTUALLY LOGICAL AND consistent perspective of the place of suffering in G-d's world. But that perspective is only part of the story, for we are not purely rational beings. We also experience the world emotionally.

Emotions are more difficult to deal with than the intellect. The emotions are unruly, often beyond our control. They cause us to react in ways at odds with our understanding. When the emotions are powerful, as they always are in the face of severe pain, they often overwhelm our intellect.

Our pain can cause us to respond to extreme suffering by railing against G-d and His justice, by denying our obligation and loyalty to Him, or even by denying His very existence. Yet deep within us, there is a central core that seeks to preserve our relationship with G-d and that rejects the words coming out of our mouths.

Railing against G-d does not solve any of our problems. Worse, if our protests are true, then our suffering is increased immeasurably. For if G-d is indifferent to us and our pain, then our suffering is meaningless. Believing that would be the greatest pain of all.

Judaism acknowledges the power of our emotions. Thus when we learn of an enormous personal loss, we make the blessing "*Baruch dayan ha'emes,* Blessed is the true Judge." That contrasts with the blessing we make on hearing good tidings, "*Hatov v'hameitiv,* the One Who is good and bestows good."

From a philosophical standpoint there should be no difference between good news and bad news. Everything G-d does is for the good and fits into His overall plan. True, we may not be capable of discerning how this is so with respect to particular events. But at a philosophical level, we understand our inability, as finite beings with a limited perspective, to do so.

Why, then, do we make a distinction between painful and joyous news?

Because we are not purely intellectual beings. Our emotions are no less part of us than our intellect. Our Sages, who composed the blessings, recognized that we are not fashioned to respond identically to good news and bad news. When we bless G-d as the "true Judge," we do not pretend to be happy about what we have just heard, or even to be capable of seeing the larger good to which the tragic events will lead. With the blessing we do no more than acknowledge that what has happened was decreed by G-d and that His judgment is not random. Our Sages recognized that no more could be demanded of us in the face of tragedy than a statement of faith. We are not required, however, to deny emotional reality.

We find in the Torah the same sensitivity to our emotional makeup. A woman who gave birth was required, in the time of the Temple, to bring a sacrifice. The Talmud states that this sacrifice was to atone for a vow that she presumably made while in the throes of childbirth to never again have a child (*Niddah* 31b). Once the agony of childbirth is past, and she is rejoicing with her new baby, she regrets the vow. The Torah recognizes that during difficult periods of extreme pain and fear, we may act in a manner which does not reflect our essential self, and therefore provides a way of removing the consequences of our emotions.

In general, the Torah does not hold one fully accountable for the vows he makes under pressure. G-d knows that under duress there is little a person can do to control his emotions. We are not expected to be able to push the pain aside, recognize that a higher purpose exists, and hold ourselves aloof. That would be unrealistic. G-d, in effect, tells us, "In moments of pain, you will lash out; you will say things, and you may even be absolutely convinced at that moment that they are true. But when the pain subsides, you will have the inner peace which will allow you to touch a deeper part of yourself and realize that what you said is not the way you really feel, that you do not believe what you said. And I don't take those statements made in the throes of intense pain as representing you."

I am not suggesting that we should feel free to say whatever we want. The new mother who made an improper vow must still atone for it, but the fact that the Torah created a ready avenue for that atonement reflects G-d's understanding of the power of our emotions. Since the Torah does not hold us strictly accountable for our thoughts in times of extreme stress, we should not compound our difficulties by berating ourselves and feeling overly guilty.

Nevertheless we are not powerless to control our emotions. Intellectual understanding that helps us frame our situation can also help guide our emotional response. Formulating a constructive vision of suffering that helps us place our suffering in the context of the future helps us avoid reacting with excessive anger. Recognizing that suffering is not G-d taking revenge against us helps us avoid feeling rejected and victimized by G-d.

Often our greatest suffering comes from the loneliness and emotional pain of feeling abandoned by G-d more than from the actual physical agony we are experiencing. When we fail to understand G-d's intentions, we run the risk of lashing out at Him. Recognizing that punishment is constructive, not vengeful, and remembering that much suffering may have nothing to do with our personal wrongdoing, helps remove the sense of rejection. All G-d's reactions are based on love. Sometimes that love is expressed in pleasant ways; sometimes it is expressed in ways that try us to the maximum.

Few of us, however, possess sufficient intellectual clarity to completely control our emotions, especially when the suffering is most intense. We lose control, and we do things that we regret later. G-d, however, understands that our emotions have the power to overwhelm us, and the Torah makes provisions for this.

What good does it do to understand the reasons for suffering if, at the crucial moment, we cannot control our thoughts? The answer is that the reservoir of understanding that we build up in moments of less intense pain provides us with something to fall back upon — a floor beneath which we will not sink, even in the worst of times.

USING OUR SUFFERING AS A MEANS OF GROWTH, OR AT least coping with suffering in such a way that it does

Life as a Gift

not totally distort our personality, is a daunting challenge. The force with which pain invades our consciousness threatens to overwhelm everything else. Only if suffering can be placed within the context of our entire existence can it be managed. To do so requires a change in our attitude towards life in general, not just our attitude towards suffering.

In general, we tend to focus on the things that we lack rather than appreciate what we have. We are conditioned to concentrate on what we are missing. Everything we receive, we immediately consider ours by right. We take it for granted and shift our focus to the next thing to be acquired.

When we suddenly lose something as important as our pain-free existence, we can think of nothing else. At precisely that moment, we have to learn to do something we should have done all along: to appreciate what we do have and to recognize that these things are gifts, not ours by right. Then what we are missing can be placed in proper perspective among all the things we have received.

We tend to assume that whatever we were born with is ours, and that we own it. When, decades later, G-d begins to tamper with our lives, we think He is stealing from us. He is unjust!

Such an attitude arises from a mistaken premise. Recall the blessing we make upon hearing of the loss of a loved one, "*Baruch dayan ha'emes*, Blessed is the true Judge." That blessing is preceded by an introductory paragraph containing the words of Job, "*Hashem nasan v'Hashem lakach*, G-d gave and G-d took back" (*Job* 1:21). When we view our lives, we must constantly be aware that each breath is a new gift of life.

Life comes without any guarantees. Our very existence requires the constant input of the Creator.

Just because I was alive yesterday is no reason that I should be alive today. The first thing a Jew says when he wakes up in the morning is, "*Modeh ani l'fanecha,* I give thanks before You ... for returning to me my soul." We did not deserve to be born, and every moment of life which follows our birth is equally a gift. Imagine how grateful we would have been had we been aware of our life as a gift at that first moment of existence. We should be that grateful every moment.

If we were fully aware of our lives as a gift, we would celebrate every moment. In the midst of celebrating, we would be too overwhelmed with gratitude to focus on what we're missing. We should tell G-d every day, "I don't know why I was born. I don't know what I did to deserve this day. If I awake to another day, I will thank You again for what I have been given."

The awareness that G-d gives us our lives provides us with the strength to deal with the times when G-d takes back. We do not own our lives. Life is a gift from G-d. Acknowledging our dependence on the Creator is a humbling experience. Yet just that humility is required in order for us to change our attitude to life and thereby place our suffering in perspective.

IF LIFE IS A GIFT, WHAT SHOULD BE OUR RELATIONSHIP TO THE Giver? What do we owe Him in return?

Life as Agency

The answer to these questions depends on our understanding of the form of the gift. Is it a one-time gift or is it a constantly renewed lease? If the latter then we are totally dependent on G-d every minute. Nothing is ours. We owe Him everything.

The Torah takes the second view. Our lives are renewed every moment. We are not private citizens, who need do nothing more than make an occasional show of obeisance to the authorities. Rather we are granted life for a purpose, and the possibility of achieving that purpose justifies our continued existence. Though there is reward, principally in the World to Come, that reward should not be the motivation for our Divine service.

We should relate to our lives as we do to work. At work we do not expect to chat with our friends on the phone, watch movies, or conduct our personal affairs. Our time belongs to the boss. He is paying us for our work. Similarly, our time in this world is G-d's. He not only grants us life; He sustains it every moment. We exist only for Him.

Our inability to endure suffering arises principally because we have our own agenda for our lives. We resent our suffering because it prevents us from accomplishing what *we* want. But if we redefine ourselves exclusively as agents of G-d, that resentment disappears. G-d gives us life, and He decides what we should do with it. Viewing matters in this fashion does not remove the pain of suffering, but it takes away our resentment of G-d for interfering with our plans.

We cannot even turn to G-d and say, "Why have You put this obstacle in my path? I could accomplish so much more without it." Our primary task in this world is to grow. The travails that we must endure are nothing more than opportunities for development. In the midst of our suffering, the most we can do is say to G-d, "I do not know why You are inflicting me with so much pain. But if I am going through this, I must need it for my unique role in history." That is the real meaning of the blessing "*Baruch dayan ha'emes,* Blessed is the true Judge." With these words, we accept that whatever befalls us has a reason.

The definition of a *tzaddik* is one who most fully views himself as G-d's agent in this world. He readily accepts suffering because he understands that he exists only for G-d's sake.

Unlike the *tzaddik*, most of us live for ourselves, and as a consequence, we have difficulty becoming reconciled to suffering. To deal with suffering, we need to develop our consciousness of life as an ongoing gift. To the extent we develop and integrate this consciousness, we will increase our ability to bear our suffering.

13

TRUST IN G-D

SUFFERING CAN LEAD US TO CRY OUT AGAINST G-D. Though deep down we believe in the Creator, our pain awakens emotions over which we have little control. Though G-d understands our limitations, still we would obviously prefer that our faith in G-d's righteousness was not overwhelmed by a welter of emotions.

King David was one who found the strength to restrain himself and not speak out against G-d. King David was hunted by his own subjects; his son tried to usurp his crown; he lost children in his lifetime. He could have voiced many complaints against G-d. Yet he says: "I will guard my ways from sinning with my tongue, I will guard my mouth with a muzzle, even while the wicked one stands before me" (*Psalms* 39:2).

Though his heart "burned" (Ibid v. 4) with doubts, King David did not give voice to those doubts. In the presence of the wicked, he muzzled himself so as not to give them ammunition against G-d. How did he restrain himself? King David himself provided the answer: "Hashem, let me know my end and the measure of my days that I might know how frail I am" (Ibid v. 5). Through humility and awareness of G-d's greatness, King David silenced himself.

Most of us are not on the level of King David. Must we then vent our anger by crying out against G-d? No. While it is natural, when caught up in pain, to be beset by doubts, our questions of faith do not have to be questions *against* G-d. They can be questions *to* G-d. We can take all the pain and all the anger and cry out, "It is not that I do not believe in You, but You have made it so hard. Please, help me understand why I am living through this. What is this all about?" We can share our pain with G-d.

When we share our suffering with G-d, we bring Him into our lives in a way that was not possible so long as everything was going smoothly. If we open ourselves up to Him, even when we do not understand what is happening to us, we forge a bond much deeper than that achievable by intellectual clarity alone. We build a bond of trust.

We began our inquiry by admitting the limits of our understanding. We can grasp the general principles of why G-d allows suffering in the world, but never know their specific applications. We can never fully answer the question, "Why me?"

A finite being by definition cannot comprehend the Infinite Mind of the Creator. We are encouraged to apply our intellects to the maximum extent possible, but we have to know that some answers will be denied to us.

Above all, suffering demands of us trust. As we said at the outset, trust is the basis of any true relationship. Were we to relate to G-d solely through our intellectual comprehension, the relationship would end each time something was beyond our understanding. But we are not only intellectual beings, and G-d seeks more than that we relate to Him through our minds. He created the world in such a way that we could relate to Him in all our wondrous complexity.

Suffering is the birthing stool upon which a true relationship with G-d is born. Only when we accept our relationship with G-d, regardless of our lack of understanding, does that relationship become as real and as deep as our own existence. At that point, our suffering occurs within the context of our relationship with G-d rather than fomenting rebellion against Him. The suffering brings us to a deeper level of relationship than was previously possible.

Rebbe Nachman of Bratslav provides an example of someone who absorbed all the pain that life can deal out, and plowed it back into an ever deeper relationship with G-d: "Elusive and so very deep; who can fathom it?" (*Ecclesiastes* 7:24). He reached remarkable spiritual heights through his personal suffering by channeling his pain into prayer. His prayer stands as a model of how we too can use our suffering to be reborn:

Awesome Holy One, please keep me from trouble and affliction. Be with me constantly. If, Heaven forbid, Your Divine justice and goodness ever require You to send me suffering, give me the strength and understanding to look for its ultimate purpose. Let me totally merge with You at the moment of pain. Let me make myself into nothing and shut my eyes to this world and its desires, until I can look into the distance and glimpse the true, eternal goal. Let the suffering bring me to this vision and, with the attainment of that vision, let all my suffering disappear... Give me the ability to ... receive any suffering that has to come to me with love and joy, transcending the pain through submission to the ultimate goal, which is wholly good. Let me receive and draw forth the waters of Torah through the joy that comes from the trace self that still remains after this experience of complete surrender.

APPENDIX
THE HOLOCAUST

NY ATTEMPT TO DISCUSS SUFFERING MUST CONFRONT THE Holocaust. The Holocaust continues to touch all of us either directly or indirectly. It would be the height of arrogance to offer an explanation for the Holocaust; only one blessed with prophetic insight could do that. Yet the issue cannot be avoided.

We have spoken about the victims of the Holocaust as martyrs to history, but we must not reduce the slaughter of 6 million Jews to some neat formula about the consequences of liberal humanism, or the danger of man-centered philosophies that deny G-d. True, the Holocaust revealed the capacity for evil that lies within the human heart. Yet it would be folly to read the Holocaust as no more than a particularly gruesome commentary on human nature removed from any Jewish context.

The Jewish people came into being in order to reveal G-d to mankind and to serve as a "light unto the nations." But that does not mean that if mankind careens off in the direction of atheism, *we* should be sacrificed on the altar. In trying to explain the Holocaust, we must search for some explanation within the context of Jewish history.

In the preceding chapters, we offered a number of reasons for suffering — e.g., punishment, the need to develop our potential, atonement for the sins of previous lives. For each of those who died in the Holocaust, we can assume that at least one or more of these reasons applied. Still, we cannot content ourselves with such explanations.

The Holocaust involved not only the deaths and torture of millions of isolated individuals, but the near destruction of an entire people. As such, it must be understood in the context of the Jewish nation as a whole. If nothing more than the tragic suffering of individuals was involved, how can we explain that so many were killed in the same way at the same time? If the Holocaust were only the result of cumulative sins of individuals, then why was the nation so profoundly affected and transformed as a consequence? Not every generation suffers this form of collective punishment. Therefore we must locate the roots of the Holocaust in the collective history of the Jewish people.

When we suffer as individuals, we must search for the explanations in the context of our individual lives. But G-d also deals with us as a people. And when He does, we must search for the causes on the national level.

THE TORAH DESCRIBES SITUATIONS OF NATIONAL DISASTER in sections of the *tochachah,* or rebuke, at the end of

The Torah s Perspective

Leviticus, in the Torah reading of *Bechukosai,* and towards the end of Deuteronomy, in the Torah reading of *Ki Savo.* Both sections begin with a glorious description of a redeemed world in which the Jewish people fulfills all its obligations to G-d. We will enjoy health and wealth; we will be spiritually uplifted; the land will be fruitful and blessed. That vision is then supplanted by one of a world in which we have turned our backs on G-d. G-d's wrath, we are warned, will express itself in horrific national suffering.

The Biblical commentators ask why such a painful description appears twice in the Torah. Nachmanides answers that these two portions of the Torah deal with two distinct events. The first *tochachah* foresees the destruction of the First Temple. The second predicts the destruction of the Second Temple and all subsequent national catastrophes. A Holocaust survivor once told me that when they read these sections of rebuke during the Holocaust, they would nod to each other in recognition that they were experiencing each of the afflictions foretold.

When we approach the subject of the Holocaust, we must remember that such national tragedies have long been part of our history, and that the destruction visited upon us was clearly predicted in the Torah.

When the sections of rebuke are read publicly in the weekly Torah portion it is customary for the *ba'al korei*, or reader, to read quickly and in a low voice. One of my great teachers, Rabbi Yitzchak Hutner, said that if he had the power he would annul this custom. Reading it softly creates a distorted viewpoint. It causes us to think of punishment as an embarrassing expression of G-d's will, as something we would rather forget. National disaster, however, is a crucial aspect of G-d's relationship with us. We must look to the Torah for an understanding of national disaster and in order to place those disasters in the context of our ongoing relationship with G-d.

The Holocaust was clearly prophesied in the Torah. Not, of course, its precise date nor the exact name of our tormentors. But the identifying circumstances are there. More important, the purpose of the tragedy is revealed.

There is a strange verse at the end of the *tochachah* in Leviticus: "But despite all [the punishments which I am foretelling], while they will be in the land of their enemies, I will not have been revolted by them nor will I have rejected them to obliterate them, to annul my covenant with them — for I am Hashem, their G-d" (*Leviticus* 26:44). Coming as it does on the heels of an extended prophecy of woe, this verse is puzzling. After all the Divine wrath and devastating punishments, how can G-d say He will not destroy us?

Rabbi Meir Simchah HaKohen of Dvinsk, one of the great scholars of the last 150 years, points out in his famous commentary *Meshech Chochmah* that there is a vast difference between suffering, pain and death that result in complete annihilation, and destruction that leaves behind something to survive and grow. The latter type of destruction is designed to produce a remnant that has been purified and strengthened. G-d never promised that He would not bring any destruction upon the Jews; He promised that He will never wipe us out entirely. Whatever destruction we suffer is not to obliterate us but to burn away a decaying shell and reveal a healthy inner body.

Rising from the Ashes

THE HOLOCAUST IS AN EMOTIONALLY CHARGED SUBJECT. IT touches most of us in a personal way. It touches me. My father, of blessed memory, was the sole survivor of his entire family. Even those who do not know someone who went through the Holocaust have likely read many memoirs of survivors and visited Yad VaShem in Jerusalem or the Holocaust Memorial in Washington, D.C.

The mind rebels at the thought that the Holocaust had a purpose consistent with G-d's love for us. Yet the Torah ends the portion of rebuke in *Leviticus* with the statement that G-d will never put an end to us. The message is that national disasters are designed to preserve us. The *Midrash* states this explicitly with reference to the portion of rebuke in *Deuteronomy*: Even though these curses fall upon you, they pre-serve you.[1]

Previously we tried to explain why death precedes afterlife by comparing the process to that of a seed,

---

1. *Midrash Tanchuma, Nitzavim* 1.

which is planted and later sprouts. The same metaphor can be applied here. Before a seed can grow into a plant it must cease being a seed. The seed must disappear before a new form can take its place. The outer portion of the seed decays to allow the essential kernel, which transforms itself into a plant, to emerge.

Destruction in Jewish history represents the decay of the outer layer of the seed, as a prelude to the transformation of the seed into something new. The old must go before the new can take its place. Whenever we turn away from G-d as a people, our former relationship with Him is destroyed, and cannot be recaptured. A new relationship, requiring a new type of people, must be forged from the ashes of the old. Destruction washes away the old embodiment of the Jewish nation. In its wake the Jewish people are reborn in a new form.

In some respects, this process parallels our understanding of the punishment of individuals. Punishment is designed to transform us. Transgression harms our relationship with G-d and causes us to turn away from Him. Subsequent Divine punishment is designed to rectify the distance from G-d, and to prepare us for reestablishing a new relationship with Him.

The paradigm for this process is Adam's banishment from the Garden of Eden. Adam was given the opportunity to live in Paradise in an intimate relationship with G-d. But he chose to remove himself from G-d by eating of the Tree of Knowledge. Afterwards, he could no longer stay in Eden. Having distanced himself from G-d, Adam needed to create a new kind of relationship. He could no longer live in the intimacy with G-d that Eden afforded. So Adam was driven out of the Garden of Eden into new surroundings in which he could develop a new relationship with G-d.

On a national level, we experienced such a transformation with the destruction of the First Temple. G-d's presence was manifest in the First Temple. Miracles were constant, and prophecy was still accessible. When idol worship penetrated society to the point that this revealed relationship with G-d was no longer possible, the Temple was destroyed, together with the entire national structure that had formed around it.

During the Second Temple period, there were no longer miracles or prophecy. Yet in that period, we experienced the flowering of the Oral Torah. Through the Oral Law, another relationship was forged between G-d and Israel very different from that which had existed prior to the destruction of the First Temple. Destruction led to transformation.

Transformation via destruction is painful, but the alternative is oblivion. The world was created so that we can enter into a relationship with G-d, and it continues to exist only for that purpose. Were we to cease pursuing that goal, or lose our capacity to achieve it, existence would come to an end.

BECAUSE THE JEWISH PEOPLE ARE G-D'S CHOSEN INSTRUMENT for bringing creation to its ultimate fulfillment they can never be destroyed. While that mission

Surviving the Cure

preserves us, it also necessitates punishments that purify us so that we can fulfill our role. On the verse, "The wicked are overturned and are no more, but the house of the righteous will endure" (*Proverbs* 12:7), the *Midrash* (*Yalkut Shimoni, Mishlei* 948) comments, "When G-d gazes upon the deeds of the evildoers and overturns them, they cannot stand ... but Israel falls and then stands, as it says, 'Do not rejoice over me, my enemy; *because* I fell, I will rise'" (*Michah* 7:8).

The first time G-d spoke to Moses, Moses saw a messenger of G-d in the midst of a burning thorn bush, "and the bush was not consumed" (*Exodus* 3:2). Moses approached the wondrous sight to find out why the bush was not consumed. G-d revealed Himself, and told Moses to return to Egypt and redeem the Jews. But we find no answer as to why the burning bush was not consumed.

The commentators explain that the burning bush was a symbol of the Jewish people. Moses was taught an essential lesson, perhaps *the* essential lesson for any leader of the Jews. Jewish history would be an ongoing story of death and destruction. But the Jewish people will never be destroyed. Indeed those destructive fires will ultimately lead to the revelation of the angel of G-d. Only through those flames will we become worthy to behold G-d. Those flames burn out the dross that enters into us, and ensure that it will never prevent us from developing a complete relationship with G-d.

RABBI MEIR SIMCHAH HAKOHEN INTRODUCED US TO THE IDEA that national catastrophe is often intended to preserve

Cycles in Exile

a strengthened remnant. He describes modern Jewish history in these terms.

For the last 2,000 years of exile, writes Rabbi Meir Simchah, Jews have moved from country to country. Jews arrive in each new country broken, destitute, and ill-adapted to the new environment. They do not speak the language or know the local customs. Strangers in a strange land, they are despised by the local population. Yet within one generation, Jews have begun to adjust to their new abode. They prosper and become more comfortable. Success is not necessarily confined to physical things: Often a renaissance of Jewish thought follows. Some of the greatest products of Jewish intellectual and cultural history have been achieved in exile. The Babylonian Talmud, for example, was produced in exile.

According to Rabbi Meir Simchah, every generation has a certain drive to outdo the past. In the world at large, this urge expresses itself in material advance and in the constant growth of secular knowledge, science, technical expertise, and efficiency.

Though this striving to outdo the past can produce positive results, it is not intrinsically positive. Our life as a nation began at Sinai with the receipt of the Torah. When we still lived in our Land, with the Temple, the *Urim V'Tumim* of the High Priest, and with thousands of prophets in our midst, our understanding of G-d's will was received directly from Him. But from the moment we were exiled from our Land, that form of knowledge ceased. Every generation is further removed from that Sinai. Our challenge is to maintain the vision of Sinai and to make the original Revelation alive for us today, even as the memory of that unique Revelation becomes increasingly refracted.

In the Jewish vision of time, we are constantly moving away from the clearest, most direct source of knowledge. That view is diametrically opposed to the Western vision of progress towards ever greater knowledge. The contrast between these two visions is nicely captured by the following story. Rabbi Yaakov Kamenetsky once found himself on an El Al flight seated next to Yerucham Meshel, who was then the director-general of the Histadrut Labor Federation. Throughout the flight, Reb Yaakov's son and several grandchildren continually visited him to ask whether he needed anything. Meshel was taken aback by the honor shown to Reb Yaakov, and confessed that he saw his own children only rarely and his grandchildren almost never. Reb Yaakov explained the difference in their relationship to their offspring in terms of their differing perspective on history. "In *your* son's eyes you are one generation closer to a monkey. In *my* son's eyes, I am one generation closer to Sinai," Reb Yaakov said.

The drive to surpass the past exists in every generation. In the Jewish context, it expresses itself among the first generation in a new country in energetic efforts to rebuild the Jewish community physically and culturally. When the generation is still downtrodden and lacks the resources for the growth of general culture and learning, the desire to outdo the preceding generation may express itself in a renaissance of Jewish culture and scholarship. But once that is accomplished what is left?

According to Rabbi Meir Simchah, the urge for new conquest is too frequently expressed as rejection of the past. A younger generation that recognizes it has no hope of attaining the depth and breadth of Torah learning of former generations abandons the Torah as antiquated. Unable to satisfy their need for achievement within Torah, members of the new generation disdain it in favor of "modernity" and "progress." That rejection begins a process of assimilation to the host culture.

G-d, however, cannot permit His people to assimilate completely into the host culture. He requires Israel's continued existence to reveal His will to the world. So G-d turns the host nation upon the Jews to remind us that we are a nation that dwells apart. We are banished and move on to another land to start the whole process over again. The process is not exactly the same each time. With each cycle, something is gained. Progress is made towards our future goals. But, to us, it seems we are starting all over — once again impoverished, once again strangers in a foreign land.

Rabbi Meir Simchah describes a general historical phenomenon. But he also had a specific example in mind: German Jewry from the eve of the Emancipation to the twentieth century. Rabbi Samson Raphael Hirsch, the preeminent figure in nineteenth-century German Orthodoxy, relates how on Tishah B'Av night of 1828, the rabbi of a small town in southern Germany ordered the local temple brilliantly lit up and his congregants to attend in their finest clothes. When the congregants were duly assembled, the preacher mounted the pulpit to protest against the mourning and sadness traditionally associated with the day. He accused all Jews still in mourning of treason and enmity toward the state and fatherland, and called upon his congregants to demonstrate by means of festal celebration their repudiation of the out-of-date yearning for

Palestine. Jerusalem, he said, was here. Palestine was now situated on German soil.

Surveying the state of German Jewry of his day, Rabbi Meir Simchah accused the Jews of Germany of mistaking Berlin for Jerusalem, and predicted that their confusion would lead to another national catastrophe. He saw the coming catastrophe as part of a long pattern of G-d acting to prevent us from committing national suicide by visiting upon us fierce anti-Semitism. Nothing so reinforces our national identity as rejection by our hosts. Rabbi Meir Simchah died in 1926, and he wrote all this in *Meshech Chochmah* decades earlier.

G-D'S CONCERN WITH PRESERVING THE SEPARATE IDENTITY OF the Jewish people goes back to the beginning of our

From the Dawn of History

history. According to the *Midrash* (*Vayikra Rabbah* 32:5), the Jews were redeemed from Egypt because they did not change their names or their language. Another *Midrash* relates that when the Jews were crossing the Sea, the nations of the world (or, in one version, Satan, the prosecuting angel) complained about the manner in which G-d saved the Jews and slew the Egyptians: "These [i.e., the Egyptians] worship idols and these [i.e., the Jews] worshipped idols," they charged (*Yalkut Shimoni, Shemos* 23).

The Jews worshipped idols in Egypt. They rejected the most fundamental tenet of the Torah. But they were nevertheless redeemed because they had not changed their names or dress. Idolatry is forbidden even to non-Jews, and the prohibition against idolatry is one of three cardinal sins for which a Jew must allow himself to be killed rather than transgress. On the other hand, there is no prohibition against changing one's name. So how could refraining from doing something that was not even forbidden have protected us from punishment for such a serious sin?

Rabbi Meir Simchah answers that for a Jew in exile the most fundamental task is the preservation of his Jewish identity. A Jew, even after he has sinned, is still a Jew. He may yet repent. But once he loses all sense of who he is, he is cut off, without a future. As long as the bulwarks against assimilation are in place and standing strong, G-d can be patient. But when Jewish identity declines, the threat of national extinction looms. Then G-d must administer bitter medicine because the entire future of the Jewish people, and through them all mankind, is at stake. The Jews in Egypt had sunk to a very low level, even worshipping idols, but they were still worthy of redemption because they maintained their separate national identity and did not change their names or dress.

Another *Midrash* highlights the connection between national identity and preservation from G-d's wrath (*Shemos Rabbah* 21:7). The *Midrash* relates that precisely at that moment when the prosecuting angel was demanding that the Jews be drowned together with the Egyptians because they too were idol worshippers, G-d distracted him by handing over Job.[2]

---

2. This *Midrash* is discussed in the *Meshech Chochmah* to *Exodus* 12:22.

Satan claimed that Job's righteousness was purely a function of the fact that he had been favored with every form of worldly success: wealth, children, good health. If those things were taken away, Satan argued, Job's faith would disappear too. G-d gave Satan permission to test Job at precisely that moment, according the *Midrash*, so that He could save the Jews at the Sea without being challenged by Satan.

Meshech Chochmah (loc. cit.) asserts that while Job observed the Torah, he did not establish "fences" designed to distance him from evil. Job's failure to institute and observe such prohibitions were considered to be evidence of some lack in his commitment — and that constituted his point of vulnerability.

As was noted, the Jews in Egypt had instituted "fences" — the customs designed to keep them separate and distinct from the Egyptian neighbors. Because they took steps to maintain their separation, they merited to be redeemed, even as Job suffered his afflictions.

Indeed, the Talmud (*Avodah Zarah* 36a) tells us that the rabbinical prohibitions designed to maintain the distinction between Jews and non-Jews, such as those against the drinking of gentile wine — the so-called "Eighteen Ordinances" — are considered so important that they cannot be annulled until the Messiah comes. Even if Elijah were to come and announce the Messiah's imminent arrival, he would not be allowed to nullify these prohibitions. Until the advent of the Messiah, we learn, the threat of assimilation and the loss of a distinct Jewish identity looms so large that it must be guarded against at all costs.

RABBI MEIR SIMCHAH MAKES CLEAR THAT CATASTROPHE IS THE Divine response to national rot that threatens to destroy

The Surviving Remnant

the existence of the Jewish nation as a distinct people. From that catastrophe, a remnant remains from which the nation can be rebuilt.

As we have seen, the Holocaust was the culmination of a long period where G-d suspended His judgment. He permitted mankind to experience a world from which He had been excluded, as it were, and to taste the fruit of the Enlightenment's confidence in unfettered human reason. Jews embraced secular liberalism as a ticket out of the ghetto. They rejected an identity that separated them from their fellow men. "We no longer need Jerusalem," they believed, "because Berlin is Jerusalem." Had the rest of mankind forgotten G-d, but not the Jews, the Holocaust would never have happened.

Yet, if assimilation was primarily a phenomenon of German Jewry, why did millions in Eastern Europe have to die as well? Why did so many of our greatest Torah scholars perish?

The truth is that the situation in Germany was only the most extreme example of a problem that had crept into Jewish life everywhere. A survivor from Warsaw once told me that the decline in religious observance between the two world wars was so precipitous that we seemed destined for a national tragedy. The threat of a complete loss of national identity existed everywhere, even if the most obvious expression was in Germany and Western Europe. G-d's response was to show the world, and the Jewish people in particular, that the culture viewed as the epitome of sophisticated humanism could turn into a ravenous beast, and that any attempt to create a man-based system of ethics and morality is doomed to failure.

Rabbi Yitzchak Hutner used to tell the following story to illustrate how thin the patina of civilization is. He recalled that as a student in the Slabodka Yeshiva, he once had a fierce argument with another student, who was filled with praise for the ethical refinement of the Germans. His friend could not get over the fact that when one asks a German for directions, he will inevitably conclude his directions with a question: *Nicht wahr*, Is it not so? He explained that the Germans do that so that the one seeking information will not feel inferior to the one who provides it. Rabbi Hutner maintained, however, that the question was a meaningless social form.

Years later, long after Rabbi Hutner was Rosh Yeshiva of Yeshiva Rabbeinu Chaim Berlin in America, his old friend from Slabodka Yeshiva came to visit him. He began by asking Rabbi Hutner whether he recognized him. The question was no formality, as the man had survived the war in the concentration camps and bore no resemblance to the young yeshiva student he had been when he had last seen Rabbi Hutner.

After identifying himself, the man continued, "You were right, and I was wrong." Rabbi Hutner had no idea what he was talking about. His friend continued, "Don't you remember the argument we once had about the morality and culture of Germany? I criticized you as a narrow-minded bigot for your stubborn refusal to acknowledge the virtue of the Germans and seeming unwillingness to praise virtue wherever it is found.

"Well, I had occasion to think back to that conversation many times in the camps," the man said. He then described an incident in the camps, where he had been ordered by the camp commander to strike a fellow inmate with a club for some minor infraction. He gave his fellow Jew a weak tap, and was ordered to strike him again. Once again, he did so weakly. At that point, the commander grabbed the club and cudgeled his helpless victim to the ground. "That is how one strikes a Jew. *Nicht wahr?*" said the commander.

WE ARE STILL CONFRONTED BY THE QUESTION: WHY WAS THE toll so high among the greatest Torah scholars and the

The Sanctification of G-d s Name

most righteous? The answer, as we discussed earlier, is that when G-d must administer strong medicine, He administers it to the strongest part of the collective body, the limb least likely to be destroyed by it.

Though the righteous individuals who perished were also needed to guide the post-operative transformation of Jewish life, first the medicine had to be given. Those who had most faithfully maintained their identity as Jews became the sacrifices for the nation as a whole, which was in a headlong flight from its own identity. That was the bitter dose.

In general, the command to save a life overrides all Torah commandments, except for the case of three cardinal sins. If one is stranded on a desert island, for instance, and the only available food is non-kosher, he is required to eat rather than starve to death. There is, however, an exception to this rule: If a tormentor demands that we transgress the commandments or be killed, with the express purpose of causing us to forswear our religion, and there are ten Jews present, then we must sanctify G-d's name and be killed. And when Jews are being persecuted *qua* Jews, we must accept death even when no other Jews are present (*Rambam, Yesodei HaTorah* 5:3).

In the situation where we are required to sacrifice our lives to sanctify the Name of Heaven, we thereby acknowledge that our lives belong to G-d and that we have no other task than to reveal His will to humanity. We do not simply work for G-d; we are His. Our relationship with Him is not like that of two friends, which can be terminated at will by either party. We cannot end our relationship with G-d. Were that relationship to cease entirely so too would we cease to exist. And what is true for us as individuals is true for the Jewish people as a whole. The Jewish people came into being through a covenant with G-d, and we continue to exist only by virtue of that commitment.

The prelude to the Holocaust was widespread assimilation, a collective turning of our backs on G-d. The righteous did not do so. They understood what their fellow Jews did not: We exist as a people only to sanctify G-d's name, and as such there is no limit on the extent of our obligation. That obligation is not a part-time one. We are not in a position to tell G-d: Until here and no further.

We have testimony from the Holocaust of the last minutes of some of the greatest Jewish leaders and scholars and how they conducted themselves.[3] They saw their role with a clarity that borders on the prophetic. One of the most moving of those testimonies concerns the final moments of Rabbi Elchonon Wasserman in the Kovno ghetto, just prior to a major Nazi liquidation action in the ghetto.

Reb Elchonon addressed those who were gathered with him. He spoke calmly, with complete serenity of spirit. His voice did not waver, and his serious mien was no different than that which he always wore. He spoke not to those who were with him as individuals, but to the entire Jewish nation. He did not even take a moment to say a personal good-bye to his son Naftali, who was together with him.

"Apparently they consider us *tzaddikim* in Heaven," Reb Elchonon began, "for we were chosen to atone for *Klal Yisrael* with our lives. If so, we must repent completely here and now. ... We must realize that our sacrifices will be more pleasing if accompanied by repentance and we shall thereby save the lives of our brothers and sisters in America." He instructed all those present to purge their minds of all impure thoughts, lest their sacrifice be invalidated.

Then Reb Elchonon addressed G-d directly, "With fire You send destruction in our midst and with fire You will rebuild the Jewish people." His last words to his students were, "The fire is about to engulf our bodies; that very fire will return and build the House of Israel."

Reb Elchonon understood clearly that the Holocaust was punishment of an entire nation, not of

---

3. See above (Chapter 8) for an account of Rabbi Daniel Movshowitz's last speech to the men of the Kelm Talmud Torah.

millions of isolated individuals. A generation was sacrificed in order to build a more solid foundation upon which to rebuild the Jewish nation.

We are still in the early stages of the recovery. Massive changes have taken place in the Jewish people since the Holocaust. The Land of Israel has been resettled for the first time in nearly two thousand years. The study of Torah has enjoyed a resurgence unimaginable in the immediate aftermath of the Holocaust, which wiped out virtually all the former centers of learning.

It is too early to predict with assurance how our relationship with G-d has been altered by the experience of the Holocaust. But it should be clear that the memory of that awful tragedy obligates each and every one of us to participate in the process of rebuilding. In particular, we must guard against extracting from the Holocaust the message summarized in the slogan "Never Again!" — i.e., we must be militarily and physically strong in order to ensure that such a tragedy never again occurs.

The Holocaust was the Divine response to a spiritual failure on the part of the Jewish people, an accelerating drive to disappear among the nations of the world. The cause was spiritual, and not physical, and so must the cure be spiritual and not physical. The Holocaust was an attack upon us as Jews, led by that nation in whose midst we were so eager to lose ourselves. As such, it serves as a constant reminder of the necessity of preserving our unique identity as a people.